HOW TO
WIN
IN REAL ESTATE

THE ULTIMATE GUIDE
FOR   REALTORS

CAMERON VAN KLEI

 FriesenPress

One Printers Way
Altona, MB R0G 0B0
Canada

www.friesenpress.com

ISBN
978-1-03-831122-1 (Hardcover)
978-1-03-831121-4 (Paperback)
978-1-03-831123-8 (eBook)
978-1-03-831124-5 (Audiobook)

1. BUSINESS & ECONOMICS, REAL ESTATE

Distributed to the trade by The Ingram Book Company

TABLE OF CONTENTS

PREFACE

The goal of this book is to help you ELEVATE your real estate career. This book is for new agents in the industry looking for a step-by-step guide on how to build a career. This book is also for experienced agents who want to take their business to the next level. Too many agents struggle in this industry: either they can't find enough business to survive, or they are overwhelmed and sacrifice family, health, free time, and sanity to chase the next sale. It doesn't have to be that way. Real estate is the best job in the world. If done properly, you can have it all: time with family, wealth, good relationships, and the freedom to do what you want. This book is full of practical tips and hard-won experiences that I have gained in my seventeen years in the industry. Following the advice found in these pages will help move you toward the professional and personal life you have always wanted.

INTRODUCTION

I am going to let you in on a little secret. Real estate is hard. Like, *really* hard. The moment you get your license and with no training or direction at all, you are now the CEO of sales, marketing, finance, client relations and everything else. From the outside, real estate is shiny and sexy. Most people think getting their real estate license means driving a Land Rover, taking exotic vacations, and being with your spouse and kids all day. The reality could not be further from the truth for most people.

I will never forget my first day in real estate. I was so excited! I had just passed the exam by one percent, and I sat down with the owner of the largest real estate company in my town. In five minutes, the paperwork was done, and I was an agent with his company. Then, the craziest thing happened. He sat forward and said "Well, go get 'em! You got this! The phone is in the bullpen!" I wandered into the bullpen—an open room with phones and computers where realtors work if they don't have an office. I stood there feeling lost, alone, and afraid, and had zero idea what I was supposed to do. There was no boss over my shoulder telling me what to do, there was no handbook of how to be a realtor, no step-by-step guide. So I sat down in the bullpen, smiled at the other realtors, and stared at the phone. It was paralyzing. I had no idea what to do next. The phone in front of me suddenly seemed like the scariest thing in the world. Who was I going to call? What was I going say? Do you just call random numbers and ask people if they need a realtor? This isn't what I signed up for. So I did what every new realtor does: I got a coffee, walked around the office for five minutes and went home because I had no boss telling me that I had to stay. Unfortunately, my experience is shared by thousands in our industry.

To say I struggled for the first few years would be an understatement. I did so many things wrong and seemed to learn everything the hard way. However, I worked hard, I was consistent, and I was willing to learn from anyone who would give me the time. Now, seventeen years later, I am writing this book because I want our industry to do better. New realtors should not have to fumble around in the dark waiting for their cousin to call and say they want to buy a house. With the right direction, advice, and support, anybody can have a successful real estate career.

Let's start by defining what I mean by "success." I believe that a successful real estate agent will be someone who gets to enjoy their friends and family, live a life of adventure, and have the freedom to set their own rules. And if you become a financially independent millionaire in the process, all the better!

This book will be much more authentic than most self-help books. It will serve as a guide for all realtors, whether they are on "day one" or "year twenty" in the business. You will hear all the mistakes I have made along the way so that you can learn from them. If you work hard and consistently, and apply everything this book has to offer, you will see your career and your life improve.

But first, let me tell you who I am. I am not a celebrity. I am the first realtor in my family, and I am not from a big expensive city. Like many of you, I am the second generation of an average, immigrant family. Being "average" held me back from writing this book for a long time. I thought I needed to be what Lebron

James is to the NBA or what Jimi Hendrix is to the guitar before I could add value to my industry. What I have learned, however, is that as long as the person teaching has achieved a level of success in their given industry, you can learn from them. I know that you are probably just like me and want to learn from people who are better than you at your chosen field.

Recently, I attended a seminar that I flew across the continent to attend. One workshop was labelled "How to Sell Homes through TikTok." The presentation was fine, but something seemed off to me, like the speaker was saying one plus one equals three and everyone was agreeing. At the end of the presentation, the speaker asked if there were any questions. I put my hand up and politely asked: "How many homes did you sell last year?" The presenter seemed offended as did half of the room. She didn't give an answer but instead told me about an award she had won. Not wanting to be offensive, I said, "great job" and didn't ask anything else. But now I was on a mission. Was she for real? Is she *actually* selling a bunch of homes per year or is she full of BS? So I did a little research and found her stats. She had sold five homes in the past year. I had flown across the country to "learn" from someone who is at the bottom of our industry. I don't think I am alone in my desire to learn from someone who is way better than average. They don't have to be the best, but they better be dang good. I tell this story because it is important to recognize that success leaves clues, so before you waste your valuable time reading this book, you need to know some of the things I have accomplished in my seventeen years in this industry. I believe that you can achieve the same results if you put in the work.

In the last twelve years, I have not sold less than seventy homes per year personally, and my small team of four realtors and one assistant sold 200 properties last year. I was voted to *REP's* "30 Realtors Under 30" in Canada and put in *Investor* magazine as one of the top people to watch in real estate under

35. I also started a real estate brokerage six years ago that has grown to over 120 realtors and is one of the fastest growing companies in North America. The average agent in my office grossed $172,634 last year while the industry average is $54,300 (NAR stats 2021). Our company has sold over $1 billion dollars in real estate every year for the last three years and last year we sold $1.3 billion. I have been fortunate enough to oversee more than 7,000 transactions. I have seen and experienced some unbelievable things. On closing days, I have had clients die, others go missing, and a house lit on fire by a disgruntled seller. I have been stuck upside down in a client's basement while trying to get a listing and found myself nearly broke after my first year in the industry because I bought a sports car instead of paying my taxes. I have seen the highs, the lows, and everything in-between and this book will tell it all.

Here are a few more reasons for you to confidently read this book and follow the advice I give. I have been buying properties since I was in my early twenties at every possible opportunity. Today, my wife and I have a real estate portfolio valued at just over twenty million dollars. Last year, my wife, two kids, and I had sixteen weeks of vacation. Much of the summer was spent boating and barbequing at our waterfront home in Lake Country, and we are able to go south in the winter to our home in Southern California. I have hiked Mt. Everest base camp, paddled the headwaters of the Amazon River, and spent nights in the Arctic under the Northern Lights. I have given lots of money away to charity, and last year I ran and biked 103 km with one of my best friends to help raise just over $127,000 dollars for Vancouver's Children's Hospital. Even though I don't have to, I still work because I love this industry!

Coaching, teaching, and mentoring is my way of giving back. In my opinion, real estate is the best industry on earth if, and only if, it is done right. I list these accomplishments not to brag, but to give you the confidence that the advice and principles you will read in this book will elevate your career and impact your life in a positive way.

This book will not make you a billionaire (although I believe anyone has that ability if they desire). What it will do is show you how to have a life of freedom, control, and success. Real estate is an incredible industry where anyone can achieve the success they desire; they just need the strategies to help them get there.

I want you to know that I loathe cheesy salespeople who reek of commission breath and selfish intentions. This book focuses on mindset, consistency, and equipping you with the right tools. No scripts, no door-knocking, no cold-calling leads or any other soul-killing activities that have very little place in today's real estate world. Instead, this book will be a step-by-step guide of how to set up your career for the long haul: how to have a consistent business, the income you desire, and the life of freedom you want.

If you close this book now and choose to do this journey on your own, the stats are not in your favour. Only 20 percent of realtors who start make it to two years in the business and after five years, only 13 percent are left. I call these people real estate tourists. They stop by our industry to see what all the fuss is about, but are soon packing their bags and are off somewhere else. There are also thousands of realtors with years of experience who are still broke, still married to their phones, and still working weekends chasing the next deal.

We will look at the business from 30,000 feet, and then dive down into the nitty-gritty, day-to-day workings. If you work hard and follow the principles laid out in this book, you will have the ability to retire a multi-millionaire, live a life of adventure, and have a story you can be proud of.

Chapter 1: What's Your Why?

I have always hated this question because it feels like an accusation, like you have to defend your choice or your motives. Business gurus will ask this from the stage and your family might ask you the same thing around the holiday dinner table, looking for an answer you may not give or have. I never knew what to say, thinking that the truth, that I like what I do, was not a good enough answer.

But over time, I have learned there is huge value in this question. Answering it for yourself helps you remember the reason you get out of bed every morning and helps you withstand the rejection that is so common in this industry. Your "why" when you are twenty will be different than when you are thirty or forty or eighty, but it is important to answer this question for yourself right now. Why do you do what you do? Why did you become a realtor or why are you thinking of becoming a realtor? Remembering why you got started in real estate will help keep you going through the hard days. If you haven't had a bad day in real estate, you aren't doing it right!

I have never heard a high school graduate say, "I want to be a residential real estate agent." Most of us graduate thinking we want to be a doctor, teacher, firefighter, or nurse because the school system has not taught us anything about becoming an entrepreneur. But somehow, three million people across North America have stumbled into this industry for one reason or another and the more realtors I meet, the more I have seen how similar many of our stories are.

I am a second-generation Canadian kid from a Dutch immigrant family. My dad worked hard and built a successful construction company from the ground up. As a young kid, I would have to sweep out a house on the job site before I could go to soccer practise. When I got older, every weekend, evening, summer holiday, spring break, and winter break was spent on the job site, and I hated every minute of it! I worked hard to impress my dad, but I knew this type of work wasn't for me. As high school went on, I loved sports and kept "A" Honours in school, wanting to impress my teachers. I did what I thought I was supposed to do. I took math, science, and all the most boring classes so I could get into university. I liked helping people and wanted to be financially successful, so I went to university to become a doctor. I was still passionate about sports and didn't want to give that up, so in my first semester of post-secondary, I played on the volleyball team and started working towards a science degree. I was unprepared for the realities of being a university athlete and a science major. I travelled to different cities for games and practices while having to keep up with calculus, physics, chemistry, biology, English and labs on top of that. Soon, my head was swimming trying to remember what on earth derivatives were and why fruit flies bred so quickly. I lasted one semester and dropped out.

I was back on the construction site the next week with a new appreciation for life, which lasted until the Pacific Northwest rains started in September and didn't stop until May. Winters here are cold, wet, muddy, and downright nasty if you work outside for a living. Working forty plus hours a week, I got to fully appreciate the terrible winters and grueling days of construction. I will never forget counting the minutes to coffee break, then the minutes to lunch break, and then the minutes till the end of the day. I began going so insane that I started calculating what I was worth per minute, which led to the realization that I was shovelling dirt for twenty-eight cents a minute! Through it all though, I worked hard every day and tried to learn from everyone I could. The most important lesson I learned during this time was that I knew beyond a doubt what I did NOT want to do for the rest of my life!

Working hard in crappy conditions for low pay is what woke up my entrepreneurial spirit. While working construction, I resolved to save all the money I could for a down payment to buy a rental property. By the time I was twenty years old, I had $50,000 saved and I bought my first rental house. Three years of waking up early to be the first on the job site and the last to leave, and then back for half a day on Saturday got me my first major investment. But I still had a problem. I hated my job and didn't know what to do.

I'll never forget this life-changing day: I was digging a trench in the mud. It was pouring rain, and my hands were white from the cold and wrinkled from the rain. I was more wet from the sweat that was trapped inside my rain pants than the water falling on my head. I looked up from my shovel and this white car pulled up, an umbrella popped out of the door and this lady with high heels walked past me into the warm, dry house. I knew in that moment that THAT was what I wanted! I wanted to be dry, to drive a nice car, to talk to people, and make a lot of money selling real estate. Did I mention I wanted to be dry?

That night I signed up for a real estate course and passed it six months later. Maybe you are like me, and you started down a path that wasn't for you. Maybe you were trying to do what your parents wanted, or maybe you needed to provide for your family for a period of time. Whatever your reason, I bet you *were* like me, and at some point, getting into real estate represented hope. It represented no cap on income, it represented equal opportunity, it represented taking control of your time, and it represented helping people. This is true for me, and it is a common story for the hundreds of realtors I have sat down with in the last seventeen years. Now, when it is raining and cold, I look out my office window, grip my warm Americano Misto (yes, I am now a coffee snob) and say a little thanks to the one above for the opportunity to take control of my destiny. On other days, when a deal falls apart that took months to put together, or yet another one of my clients uses another realtor, I think to myself that it could be worse. I could be working outside in the pouring rain for twenty-eight cents a minute!

So, what's your "why"? Why did you end up in real estate? Burn the answer into your mind and use it as fuel to keep you going on the days that are downright hard. When that judgmental person at Christmas dinner asks you why you do what you do, you can give them your answer with confidence.

With your "why" clear in your mind, it is time to start or restart your career the RIGHT way, with the systems, plans and goals in place to build a strong and enduring business.

Chapter 2: 30,000 feet

In 2008 I was twenty-three years old and sitting at my desk wondering why my phone had stopped ringing. Parked outside was my new 2007 mustang GT, I had no money in my bank and a mortgage to pay. Suddenly, the phone rang, and I excitedly picked it up. "Hello, Cameron speaking." I called myself Cameron instead of Cam because I looked and sounded like a twelve-year-old, and I thought answering my phone this way made me sound older and more dignified. On the other end of the phone was not someone calling me to say they had cash in hand to buy a million-dollar home and they wanted me as their realtor. It was my accountant. After some small talk, he told me what he called "good news." My tax bill was only going to be $25,000 dollars for the year. "What?" I said. "I have to pay taxes? Don't they automatically take taxes off my commission cheques?" The accountant chuckled nervously and said, "Cameron, you are an independent contractor, which means you must pay your own taxes."

When I hung up the phone, I could feel myself starting to sweat. I had a mortgage, a brand-new sports car, no money in the bank, and the market was plummeting. Unfortunately, this is a common story in our industry. The only thing that would have made it more typical was if I had been in Vegas when I got the call. The sad reality of our industry is that business skills are completely overlooked when we get our real estate license. We think the sales will keep rolling in, and with each sale we can spend more. In this image-based industry, we think "appearing" successful is necessary, and so we spend too much money on fancy cars and vacations. The problem with this mentality is that it ruins a lot of great realtor's financial futures.

The next day, I went into my bank and got approved for, and immediately maxed out, a $25,000 line of credit to pay my taxes. The bank teller asked me what I needed it for, and I was too embarrassed to tell the truth, so I said I needed it to help me run my new real estate career. I learned some valuable lessons through this experience but at the time it was not fun.

Let's back up fourteen months from this phone call so I can prove that new agents need to learn how to build a real estate business the right way. It's the end of 2006, I am the newest realtor in my small city, and I am about to set the world on fire! It took me two long months, but I finally had my first accepted offer, on Christmas Eve, for my client, who also happened to be my best friend. What a rush! But other than begging my friends to use me as their realtor, I had no idea how to get business, so I decided open houses were my best chance. Luckily for me, my dad was a home builder, and he gave me a few listings and allowed me to do open houses whenever I wanted. I still had my day job in construction, so I worked from 7:00 a.m. to 4:00 p.m., changed into clean clothes in my car, and sat in open houses for a couple of hours every evening and every weekend. As 2007 rolled on, I thought I was God's gift to real estate. Buyers came to open houses in crowds and wanted to buy either the house we were in or one across town. I would offer them a commission kickback if they used me as their realtor. Many of them said I reminded them of their grandson and was I was even old enough to sell real estate? I assured them I was, and by the end of 2007, my first official year in real estate, I had sold 33 homes and was "rookie of the year" in the biggest company in town. I was living the life! On the outside it seemed like I had it all together. "Rookie of the Year," nice truck, fancy sports car, and I owned my own home. If you pulled back the curtain on my life even a little bit, however, you would have seen the truth: I was broke, owed on a line of credit, and had no idea how to run a successful business. I had given away most of my commissions to get those early deals and had saved nothing.

When the market slowed down in 2008, with my tail between my legs, I walked into my boss's office and told him I had no idea what to do. I wasn't selling houses anymore. Did he have any advice for me? He looked at me, reached into his drawer and handed me a CD by a sales coach named Tom Hopkins and said it might help. This turned out to be a defining moment in my career. I probably listened to that old CD a thousand times. Tom Hopkins was an old-fashioned salesman from back in the day, but the heart of what he had to say was so applicable to me and the problems I was facing. And more importantly, listening to that CD gave me the passion to learn. From that moment on, I read every book I could get my hands on and signed up for as much coaching as possible. I was learning at a feverish pace and applying everything I learned. I use these stories because I didn't know what I didn't know, at first. Just like you probably don't know. It is important to understand the fundamentals of our business from 30,000 feet before you begin building it from the ground up. This will save you time, energy, and money.

Building a mature business from the ground up doesn't happen overnight. In reality, it takes about five years for your business to reach maturity. Too many new realtors come in with the expectation of getting rich quick. Some do, but then quickly burn out and don't make it for the long haul. Others have such high expectations of themselves that they get frustrated when they don't see immediate results, get discouraged, and quit. So many agents come into my office in their first year with frustration in their eyes. I can tell they want sales NOW and it isn't happening like they thought it would. I can see the self-doubt starting to creep in. These agents will sit down and proceed to tell me that they have tried everything! They emailed the people they know, they tried five open houses, door-knocked for a week, cold-called for a week, and then bought some internet leads. They are two months in and ready to quit because no one wants to buy a house. Maybe you can relate.

My advice to those new agents, and to you, is to treat your career like a master's degree because the amount of knowledge required is incredibly high. Thinking of it like getting a degree makes sense because no one in university quits after a year because they are angry they don't have their degree yet. They understand that it takes time. If realtors had this same mentality, their expectations would be much more realistic and frustration levels would be lower. Instead of being upset at not making $100,000 their first year, they would be proud making $25,000, knowing that with a proper business plan, by year five they can be making six figures.

From 30,000 feet everything below seems so simple. Mountains seem flat and all our problems seem small. It is not until we are on the ground that the mountains seem so big, and our problems feel overwhelming. Therefore, I want to show you the big picture of building a successful business before we get busy learning all the small stuff.

The first basic principle is that real estate sales is broken up into two simple concepts: getting the business and doing the business. This is obviously very basic, but you can't do the business unless you first get the business. For the rest of your career this will be a simple break down of how to organize your day. We always need to spend part of the day getting business in order to spend the rest of the day doing the business. Getting the business is often the biggest challenge and requires the most amount of focus. This is the reason why most realtor's struggle. They lack the focus and discipline to "get the business." We always want to find the easy way out, which is why salespeople gravitate towards not doing the work to get clients. Additionally, it's easier to chase the immediate rather than putting in the work to build relationships. Realtors want sales now. This is why salespeople tend to buy leads, door knock, or do social media posts rather than spending the time to build relationships and add value. Never forget this principal! The ability to get business is the biggest separator from the top 20 percent vs the bottom 80 percent. If you are struggling now it's probably because you don't spend enough time getting business.

The next principal is learning how to structure your business. This is something I wish I had learned early in my career, but unfortunately, I wasn't that lucky. It took me a few years to figure it out, but when I did, everything changed. Setting up a mature real estate business consists of three equally important parts. Get clients. Keep clients. Get referrals. Let me say it again because it is so important. Thirty-three percent of your business should be getting clients, 33.3 percent of your business should be keeping your clients, and 33.3 percent of your business should be referrals. This system will give you structured and keep you on track to stay focused in the right areas of our business. It is such a simple formula, and I will go into great detail about each part of this structure in later chapters, but for now let me explain why this is the best strategy for building your real estate business. Getting clients in the most obvious. If we don't get new clients, we can't sell houses! Even experienced agents need fresh faces over time, or they will see their sales dwindle as former clients die, get divorced, or have family members or friends get their real estate licenses. If you aren't diligent in finding new clients, your business may go back to zero.

The second part of your structure is keeping clients (or repeat business). Unfortunately, many realtors neglect this part of their business. They get stuck in the chase: chasing internet leads, door-knocking, and doing open houses all at the expense of their past clients. Your past clients already know, like, and trust you, so doing another transaction with these clients takes very little time or money because they already trust you and will want to work with you. The average person moves roughly every five to six years; this means if you do a good job and stay in contact you will have a repeat client every six years.

The third part of your structure is getting referrals. Having this three-part structure to your business builds stability and consistency because 66 percent of the time you will be working with people who want to work with you through repeat business and referrals. After ten years, most realtors will be working with referrals and repeat buyers on 80 percent of their transactions. This happens naturally, as over time your client base grows, and you will not need to chase new business.

Using this three-part structure as the engine that drives your business will put you ahead of 80 percent of realtors in my opinion. You will not sell houses by accident or always be on the chase. You will have a consistent and trackable business that you can be certain of through good, bad, and average markets. This system can be implemented on day one or on year ten if you are an agent who is worn out from not having a plan. I have worked with many agents whose business was stable for several years but went to a whole new level once they implemented this 3-part plan.

The next principal is to understand the different stages of a real estate career and figure out where you are at. Too many realtors are in their fifteenth year in the business but have not progressed through the stages properly. They think they are experienced, but in reality, they are doing their first year for the fifteenth time. My goal is to help you move though the stages of a career so that you will have a clean reliable business that allows a life of adventure and the ability to retire wealthy. The elevation process of a career should look something like this:

The Early Years (Years 1–5)
This is where you treat your new career like a business degree. This time should be focused on learning and finding great mentors over making the most money possible. These years are spent gaining as many new clients as possible and building the best database possible. You should spend a lot of time prospecting and building relationships for the future. Many evenings and weekends will be used up for work during this period. You should be learning as much as possible, you need to become a sponge and learn from everyone you can. This is where I highly recommend hiring a coach or attending as many conferences as possible. It is better to learn the right way the first time rather that getting stuck in your ways of running a bad business with bad habits. You will be building the system: get clients, keep clients, and get referrals in your business. It is important to note that it takes over five years to get this system working for you, and that is mainly because you have to wait for the clients to become repeat buyers, which is five to six years on average.

The Early Middle Years (Years 6–10)
This is where you focus on consistency, systems, and leverage. This is the part of your career where you have now built a database and a lot of great connections. You should be able to work

as a "database realtor" and won't need to prospect as often. You will be a pro at the get clients, keep clients, and get referrals system and your income will really start to increase. You will no longer struggle with consistency in selling homes. The hours spent working will decrease and you will no longer be required to work as many evenings or weekends. This is the time where you will define your systems and start to leverage your time. This is the time when you should consider hiring an assistant. You should also start investing in real estate during this period, as you are setting yourself up to take control of your time.

Middle Late Years (Years 10–15)

These are my favourite years. At this point your business can run at a high level without as much work. Trust has been built and your referrals are high. Your database clients are happy and you don't have to compete with other agents as much. You will be working less and making more if you do it right. You should also invest in real estate and will be earning income from both sales' activity and investments. You will also become your own client during this time because you are helping yourself buy the best investments in the market. The middle years allow for vacation time and starting to enjoy the fruits of your labour. This is where you get to start living a life of adventure and freedom.

Retirement Set-up (15+ Years)

This is the time when you can go in any direction you want. If you set up your career right and implemented the right systems, then you will have a robust business. Finances won't be a major factor in your decisions, and you will truly be living a life of freedom and adventure. This is the time when you can start to build your exit strategy in the business. I believe real estate is the best job in the world and we get to bring a lot of value to many people. This is why I believe retirement isn't always necessary. If you love what you do, there is no reason to fully retire. Our industry has so many opportunities and these are best explored in these years. The earlier years require a lot of focus so you should not distract yourself with other opportunities. However, after fifteen years in the business I empower you to explore any opportunities that bring value to your life.

Now that we have reviewed the business from 30,000 feet, we are ready to move on. The next chapters will get into the nitty gritty of our business and will really help you on your journey.

Chapter 3: Get Clients

When you learn to attract business rather than chase it, your whole world will change. We all understand that we need to get clients to grow a business. Getting clients can also be called prospecting or lead generating. Personally, I don't like the word prospecting because it feels too sterile. The people we work with are humans and not "prospects" or "leads." I prefer to call the people I work with "clients" because they are people I treat with respect and people I want to do a great job for.

So where, and how do we get new clients to grow our business? This process is unique to every realtor, and you can try anything you want to. Most new agents gravitate towards cold-calling, door-knocking, or buying leads from the internet. My opinion of these activities is that they are soul-sucking, and I would never want to do them. The amount of rejection involved in these activities (you will get hundreds of nos before you get a yes) is hard on me, and unless you are super-human, I think it will be hard on you, too. For example, converting an internet lead has a success rate of under 2 percent, not to mention the fact that you must answer the lead within minutes of receiving it or you will lose it to a hungrier agent. This means you must be on the clock twenty-four hours a day if you want to convert internet leads. This is not how I want to spend my time. I think the Golden Rule applies to sales as much as it applies to life: you should treat others how you want to be treated. If I am at home with my family after a hard day of work, the last thing I want to do is answer my phone, or a knock at my door to a salesperson. If anything, it makes me angry because I value family time, and they are taking it away from me. Sadly, many agents who aren't taught how to get clients become desperate and default to the immediacy of lead generation. We live in a world of instant gratification, and I think this causes realtors to approach prospecting in the same manner. But there is another way.

First, you need to go fishing where the fish are. Whether you are new or experienced, you need to learn where the majority of the clients come from and then spend all your time there. There are three main places to find new clients: our sphere of influence (people we know), open houses, and geographical farming. These three sources account for about 90 percent of all clients that a realtor will get (stats can be found on the NAR website). With these statistics, why would you try anything else? Rather than killing your soul making cold calls, door-knocking, or buying internet leads, double down on these three higher yielding activities.

As a new realtor, I had no idea what to do and no direction from my company, so I defaulted to open houses. Open houses seemed like a place where I would meet people who were interested in buying or selling a home; in other words, potential clients would come to me rather than me chasing down leads. With lots of energy but no training and no plan, I decided to do open houses seven days a week. Life is often a numbers game, so I thought the more open houses I did, the more clients I would meet, and I was right! Almost every deal I did in the first year was from an open house and very few were from my sphere of influence (SOI).

Luckily for me, 2007 was a hot real estate market where I live. Truthfully, I was more of an "order taker" than a salesperson. People were buying quickly because they didn't want to miss out and prices were rising. They would come into the open house, tell me they wanted to buy it, I would write the contract and sell them the house. In my first year I sold thirty-three homes. Looking back, this was both good and bad for my career. It was good because I was getting the experience of writing deals, but it was bad because I was growing an ego and building bad habits. Instead of building and working a database or learning fundamental skills, I sat in open houses thinking of all the ways I could spend my new money. As fate would have it, the market crashed within the year and I found myself sitting in open houses every day with no sales skills, no plan, and no buyers. It was time to set the reset button on my career and start doing things the right way.

The Sphere of Influence Database

This is the engine that drives any successful real estate career. If you want steady sales and control over your time, your SOI is where it starts. We need to learn to work with the people we communicate with in everyday life. People want to buy from people they know, like, and trust. Commit that to memory! Think of it this way: when a family hires a babysitter for their children, often they will pick the thirteen-year-old neighbour down the street rather than a highly qualified thirty-year-old who they don't know. Isn't that crazy? What if there is an emergency? Who would you want at your house with your children, another completely unqualified kid or the fully trained thirty-year-old? Logically, we would say of course the thirty-year-old, yet we almost always hire the kid next door. The same is true in real estate. Sellers or buyers will call their cousin who got his license yesterday to help represent them in the biggest financial transaction of their life rather than someone they don't know, even a veteran agent who has sold hundreds of properties. This should encourage you! It means that you have a shot selling as many houses as a veteran agent, IF you recognize that the key is to tap into your SOI.

Setting Up Your Database

Research done by Columbia University shows that the average person knows approximately 600 people. In addition to this, the average person will meet roughly 80,000 people in their lifetime. These stats show that if you are new or want to reset your career, then you need to set up a database. I recommend picking a quiet location and not leaving until you generated 150 to 250 names from your phone contacts, social media friends, and people you are involved with in the community through school, sports, volunteer work, boards, or church. For example, I have now sold a home to almost every single one of my teachers from kindergarten through high school.

For every person in your database, you must have this information: home address, birthday, and email address. You can get more information, but this data is a great start. Next, you must have it in a central and editable format like a simple excel spreadsheet. There are many great CRM systems (client retention management), but they all change over time, so keeping something that doesn't change is very important. Once you get going on this, you will find this easier than you think to get a database of 150–250 people.

I want to break down just how effective a well-run database can be for your business because the path is in the math. The average person in North America moves every 5.7 years. Let's round up to six for easy math. If you are in connection with a database of 150 people, that means in six years on average, they will all move. They won't all move at the same time, so let's split it evenly between the six years, which means that every year, roughly twenty-five households will want to move. It follows that if they sell their home, they will also need to buy a home. So that means fifty transactions: twenty-five listings plus twenty-five sales. We should consider that some of your database won't use you and some of them will move to a different city, so let's be conservative and say 50 percent of the sales will be lost to other agents. That means you will still sell twenty-five houses that year just from your database. That is more than double the 2022 NAR reported yearly average of ten. The average commission per transaction is $10,000, which means you have grossed $250,000 from your database in one year. That is not even taking into consideration any other transactions that you will get from other sources like open houses and referrals. A database that you are in constant connection with will be a steady and reliable source of business for years to come.

Converting Your Sphere of Influence into Buyers and Sellers

Now that you have the spreadsheet, you will only get results if you do something with it. After you have a database set up, you need to master the rarely taught art of connection and conversion. People need to one, know you exist and two, want to use you as their agent. If people know you, but aren't using you as their agent, this points to problems with communication and/or consistency with your database. Whenever I meet with a struggling agent, the first question I always ask is about their database; do they have one and what do they do with it? Within minutes, I can usually tell why they are struggling, and it's almost always connected to their database. We must communicate to our sphere of influence that we exist, bring value, are consistent, and are therefore the expert they want to work with when buying or selling property. Simply shouting from the rooftop that you are a realtor is not enough. The average person knows several realtors so you need to let them know why they should choose you. The average person spends six months thinking about starting the process of buying or selling, but they only take seventy-two hours to pick their realtor. You need to be top of mind when clients are making this decision, and you can accomplish this by regularly connecting with your database.

Connection is the main reason people will work with you. The definition of connection is a relationship in which a person, thing, or idea is linked or associated with something else. What this means for realtors is that we must be the person who people associate with buying and selling property. This connection built with clients needs to be an active connection. If you had a connection five years ago, but have done nothing to keep it active, don't expect to be the realtor that connection chooses. Older realtors have come into my office complaining that their past clients are using new and inexperienced realtors instead of them. They are upset that their former clients don't remember how hard they worked to get them a good house. After a few follow-up questions, it becomes clear that the most common reason that these realtors' former clients went with a different realtor was the lack of active and ongoing connection with those past clients. How each individual builds connection is as unique as the person, but there are some steps that everyone can take to start connecting with and converting your database into clients.

Use the Mail

Step one is using the mail system to your advantage. Mail has a very high open rate and feels personal. I recommend sending your database one piece of mail every month. Connection is built through authenticity, so treat each person as unique and special in your mail communication with them.

Types of mail connections can be broken down into five types: demonstrating expertise, personal connection, items of value, evidence of success, and referrals.

1. **Demonstrating Expertise**

    This is done with well-written and well-presented market updates of the area your client lives in. My market updates show the current market stats and how they affect the different types of clients by including pros and cons for buyers, sellers, investors, upsizing, and downsizing clients. Every market is unique and presents opportunities or challenges depending on the type of client. Sometimes the market has cash flow for investors, other times it is the perfect time to downsize, and other times you should cash out. Every quarter, you should spend time thinking and researching how the current market conditions affect all your clients and then communicate this with your SOI. It only takes about forty-five minutes to write and maybe an hour more to edit to make it look appealing and professional. Every time a market update goes out, I get at least five people who want to list their homes. Not bad for under two hours of work!

    There is also a ripple-effect to these mailings. Your database will share them with their friends and family, and more people will see the value you offer as a realtor and how vast your expertise is. I have even had local schoolteachers use my market updates in class to teach business to their students. I need to stress the importance of writing the market update yourself and not letting artificial intelligence do the work for you or cutting and pasting macro stats or articles from people who claim to be economists. Remember that your purpose is to prove your own expertise while making connections with the people on your database. If you send a market update from another person, your database will see it a mile away and perhaps assume that you are not an expert since you relied on others for your content.

Your database will have everyone from first-time buyers to investors to retirees, so anything you write needs to connect with all of them. An article that relies on general stats will not connect. Even if your writing skills are poor, your own words are better than sending a puff piece, and there is always the option of asking or hiring someone with expertise to review it for you. Once you have your market update, you can also use it for drip emails, for your farm area, and for your buyer and seller presentations.

2. **Personal Connection**

Real estate agents are in the business of people, and we just happen to also sell houses. If you build connections with people, they will want to use you for their real estate transactions. If you have a strong connection with someone, you can compete with even the best agents in the world for their listing. Connection matters. Throughout the year, everyone in your database must get a handwritten birthday card, Christmas card, and if possible, a house-aversary card, which is simply a card you send on the anniversary of your clients moving into a new home. Making these connections will separate you from your competition. No one seems to mail out handwritten cards anymore, and if you do it, you will build massive rapport with your SOI. The card should be an unbranded simple card that says Happy Birthday with something you appreciate about them handwritten inside. This is not the time to shout that you are a realtor. Focus on the person and be authentically thankful for your relationship. Receiving this in the mail will be special, memorable, and impactful for your client. I also recommend a handwritten Christmas card and if you want to take this concept to the next level, you can also send out birthday cards to your clients' children.

In today's world, many people live their lives on social media, and this can be a great place to keep up to date on your clients. For example, you might see on their Facebook or Instagram account that they are retiring, and you can send them a bottle of scotch, or if they have a child graduating high school, you can send them flowers. There are so many ways you can build connections. Investing in this level of connection is why a database of two thousand people doesn't make sense because you will be unable to maintain consistent and meaningful connections with each person.

3. **Items of Value**

   Four times a year, you should send an item of value to everyone in your database. This will build connection while making them always want to open mail from you! Items of value can include your swag: pens, notepads, calendars, etc. These should be branded of course with your name and information. Some of these things are becoming a bit outdated, so I like to get creative. Often, I will send out a schedule of the local sports team to put on their fridge or a magnet that can be flipped in different directions to let them know if the dishwasher is clean or dirty. In the spring, I send all my clients some seeds for their garden, in the summer they get a free ice cream cone coupon at a local ice cream store, in the fall they get a free pumpkin, and in the winter, we give out a calendar or poinsettia. I have been doing this for several years now and it really works to bring connection and value to the relationship. You can get creative with this idea and make the items unique to you.

4. **Evidence of Success**

   Our database needs to know that we are good at what we do. It can be off-putting when a realtor tells everyone how great they are, but it's different if it's on a piece of advertising. Your SOI wants to know that you are successful (no one wants to refer a poorly producing realtor) and they will be proud of you. You need to send some evidence of success at least three times per year. At the start of every year, you can send an update of your previous year's sales, thanking your clients for being a part of your successful year. Real estate has no shortage of awards, so doing a "year in review" that includes some of your successes will be well received.

5. **Referrals**

It's important for your database and past clients to know that you are hungry and looking for business. At least twice a year, I mail what I call a referral card, which simply reminds people how much I value a referral. This card is a double-sided paper with how much I am willing to pay for a referral that leads to a sale on one side and a bit of ego marketing on the other. Your referral incentive can be whatever you want it to be. Early in my career, I would give away $2,000 per referral because I wanted as many new clients as possible, and I wanted the motivation to be high; $2,000 is obviously way too much, but it worked in the way I wanted it to at the time. After a couple of years, I dropped it to $500 dollars, and today, I pay $350 in cash for every referral that leads to a sale. Even if your past clients don't refer you, it's a good reminder to them that referrals matter to you and that you care about running a great business.

The ego marketing on the other side will include some stats or awards that you have recently won. If you are new and have no awards to speak of, you can say things that make you look good like: "I sell 95 percent of the homes I list", or that your average days to sell a home is seventeen. You can also add some testimonials of happy clients.

This referral card can be put in the same envelope as your market updates, or you can send them on their own. Doing this will help build a culture of referrals and show that other people are also referring you. I will go into greater detail about how to build a culture of referrals in Chapter 6.

In summary, do not underestimate the mail system. It is a space with little competition and very high results. I dare you to try it and tell me it doesn't work!

Drip Email

Emails are not my favourite way to connect with my database because the open rate is very low, and it doesn't feel personal. But they are effective in that they keep you on people's radar and the time commitment is low. Most CRM programs you buy will send your whole database an email on a schedule and have all the content already completed. This is good to help you stay top of mind, but unless you personalize it, your database will not trust the emails, if they open them at all. There is a big risk sending non-personalized email as too many emails may cause your clients to block you, and that would hurt your business. If someone is annoying you, it's human nature to become a bit resentful toward them. So make sure any emails you do send feel personalized and have good information that brings value to the person reading it. Many times, I will call a realtor from another city and ask to be on their email list just to see what they are doing. In my experience, sending emails with exclusive market information or sales activity close to your buyer's home are the only emails people will actually open. Remember the Golden Rule! Think about how you feel when you get junk emails from salespeople, and make sure you are not doing the same thing to your database!

Using all of these mail-out ideas will translate to sending a monthly piece of mail to everyone in your database. If you do this, I promise your business will hit a new level. You will begin to see people coming to you instead of you having to chase them. Often, I have clients call me and say, "We are so sorry to bother you, but we went to an open house this weekend, and we love it! Can you write up an offer for it and then list our house?" Of course, I say yes, and I have now sold two houses without chasing either one. This sort of thing happens only because I have an active connection with my clients, and they trust me. It sure beats knocking on thousands of doors, cold-calling, or chasing internet leads!

Join your Community

Another great way to gain new clients is to be an active member of your community. This is one of the best ways to build new and active relationships. My advice is to join things you love doing: volunteering, social clubs, athletics, boards, etc. I have seen many realtors achieve success in their business primarily by being a very active part of the community. They have no systems, no follow-up, and no business plan, but they sell a lot of houses because they are consistently in contact with a lot of people. The danger with relying heavily on this to generate new clients is that it can be an overwhelming way to live. Personally, I could not imagine being out every night and being with people 24/7 but some people are wired that way, and it works for them.

Giving you the advice to join your community to generate business makes me nervous, so here's a warning for you: I have seen too many realtors handing out business cards at church or asking people if they want to buy a home while they are running beside them in their running club. This is NOT what I am talking about. Do not be the person who is clearly involved in something for selfish gains. Our business is always relationship first, so don't forget that. We know that people in our community will move at some point in their lives and our goal is to provide great value to them when that moment comes for them. You don't have to tell people you are a realtor when you are out in the community doing what you love. Wear a bit of swag with your logo on it, and focus your energy on building good connections with people. Then, when they have a real estate related question, they will trust you enough to ask you.

My community involvement has always led to people using me as their realtor. When I was coaching basketball, I ended up selling some of my players' parents' houses. I have sold the homes of my squash league members and my fellow church-goers. Never did I actively solicit people. I was just friendly and tried to make deposits into the relationship banks of other people. I have zero expectations and am never upset if they do not use me as their realtor. When you take this approach, here's what always happens: inevitably, that person you have built connections with will ask you, "So how's the market?" If you are pushy or inauthentic, no one will ask you about the market because they won't trust you or want to hear what you have to say.

If you have ever had someone ask you how the market is, give yourself a mental pat on the back, but also be careful how you answer that question. A common mistake is to say, "It is very busy." When you say this, you are telling the person two things: One, that you are so busy you probably don't have time to add them as a client and two, since the market isn't always busy, you might sound like you are distorting the truth and lose the person's trust. You need to answer this question with either specific stats or another question. Here is how it might go:

Them: "How is the market right now?"

You: "It's really interesting! It seems to be moving from a buyer to a seller's market."

OR: "The market is good for sellers right now because the average house sells in fifteen days."

OR: "It's great for buyers because the inventory is the highest it has been in two years with around three thousand homes for sale."

OR you could ask a question: "What section of the market are you asking about?"

Any of these answers demonstrate your level of expertise and will build trust with the potential client. Instead of saying that the market is busy, say it is busy because of x, y, or z. A few examples of stats you can use to answer this question are months of inventory (MOI) for a buyer's or seller's market, unit sales, days on market, average house price, or price per sq foot. Answering the "how's the market" question this way also does another important thing: it begins a two-way conversation in which you can discover the client's reason for asking the question in the first place. Most of the time, a person asks this question because they want to buy or sell in the near future.

If you can get the conversation naturally to the place where they reveal their reason: that they are debating buying a rental or thinking of selling and buying a place with some land, or looking to downsize and travel, you will likely become their realtor of choice.

Now, remember that this conversation is taking place when you're out in the community, so at this point in the conversation the goal is to book a meeting at your office or a local coffee shop in the next two to three days (longer than this and they will have the chance to talk to several people and have other realtors recommended to them). If you can book this meeting (which will be either your buyer's or listing presentation), you will likely have converted this person into a client.

Ranking your Database

Evaluating your database is a very effective tool for getting new clients with minimal work. You need to take your database and rank them into three groups: A's, B's, and C's. As a rule of thumb, all three of these groups should receive your monthly mail plan and drip emails or whatever you decide your database system of monthly mailings will be, but the A clients will get the most focus while the C's will get the least amount of time and attention. We break them into different categories so we can better focus our time and energy on where most of our transactions will come from.

1. **A List Clients**

    Let's start with the A's, the strongest part of your database and the source of 80 percent of your business. In this group are typically influential people who are your biggest fans. The key word here is "influential." A person might be your biggest fan but not an influential person. They will tell you that they refer you constantly, but none of those referrals have ever contacted you. Your A clients are people who have done several transactions with you, but more importantly, they also create at least two transactions per year for you. This can be a construction company that builds several homes per year, or a teacher who refers several colleagues to you every year, or an investor who is always buying and selling. Ideally, you should aim for fifteen to twenty-five people in your A group. If you have twenty-five A's and you get two transactions per year from each, that is fifty deals in one year. If the average commission in your market is $10,000, then you just made $250,000 working with people you like. These people should be the main focus of your business.

    As a new realtor, finding one or two A's might be the difference between the success and failure of your business, so set out to build relationships with well-connected, influential individuals in a variety of fields. Some examples are bank managers, financial planners, business owners, drafting companies, nurses, teachers, prison guards, and companies that specialize in any kind of construction materials. All of these people are in contact with people who buy and sell homes on a regular basis, and you want them in your corner. There is a danger here of coming across pushy and cheesy, so my best advice to starting a relationship with them is to call them on the phone (not email or text) and ask them if you can take them to lunch. Tell them they are a person you respect, and you would love to get to know them better. In my experience, I am rarely rejected when I ask this, and remember to pay for lunch! If you can't afford lunch, take them for coffee.

You must have a plan for your A list. Remember these people are typically busy and have a lot of responsibility in their lives. Your goal is to stay top of mind with them through personal connection. There are three ways you can achieve this. First, let them know that they are your biggest referral source. It will make them feel special and want to refer you even more. Communicate this to them in a handwritten card or in person. Secondly, give really cool referral gifts. I have thanked some of my best clients by sending them on vacations, giving them a new ride-on lawn mower, or having chocolates delivered to their door every month for a year. If you give them a memorable gift, guess what? They will remember you. If you send a client away on a romantic weekend with their spouse for a referral, do you think they are going to keep it a secret? No way. They will tell everyone they know about their cool realtor.

Thirdly and most importantly, you must have four face-to-face connections with each person per year. This can be as simple as a coffee or lunch, or you can do an exclusive client event. I have seen some of my best agents take their twenty A list clients to sporting events or on helicopter rides. No matter what your budget is, there are creative and personal ideas that you can come up with to connect with your A clients and make them feel valued and special.

2. **B List Clients**

This group really matters! They are customers who will buy and sell with you and perhaps even give you a referral. You have a great vibe with them, and everyone enjoys the process when you work together. These people are on the B list because they will move every six years and have a lower chance of influencing their sphere of influence for referrals. You need to stay top of mind with these people as well because you never know when they may want to move again. Also, many B's have the opportunity to become A's as they get older. I have had B's as first-time buyers, but then they open a business and quickly turn into A clients. Your B's should be on your monthly mail list and drip email campaign. Additionally, I would recommend calling them at least three times per year to see how they are doing. One of those calls should be to discuss how the value of their home has changed accompanied by an email with all of the comparables in their neighbourhood. Finally, I would plan one big client event per year for all of your B's. This can be as simple as a Christmas event where you have hot chocolate and give them a poinsettia plant for their home. B's are very important clients so stay in regular contact with them.

3. **C List Clients**

These are the clients that you would be happy never to do business with again. You sold them a home, but no one had any fun. For whatever reason, trust was low, and the vibe was off. I mean no disrespect, but from a business standpoint, you should not be putting time and energy into this list. Don't burn bridges, but don't give them any of your focus. With C clients, keep them on your drip email system because you never know. Some C's can turn into B's or even A's over time so don't discount them completely. If they call you in a few years to buy or sell again, consider it a nice bonus.

The Open House

Open houses are the number two source of generating clients behind your database sphere of influence. Any agent can build a career from open houses. Young, old, experienced, or brand new in the business, it doesn't matter. I love open houses because it doesn't matter who you are, how many people you know, or how deep your database is. All the top producers I know have spent many hours in open houses.

My favourite thing about open houses is that they are an attractional activity. In other words, buyers and sellers come to you instead of you having to chase them. Every realtor who wants to increase their business and find more clients should start with an open house: it is where I built my career. It is no exaggeration to say that I have done thousands of open houses. For many years, I gained a minimum of twenty transactions per year from open houses. These open houses early in my career helped build my database. Every year, I could add twenty more people to the list of those who had trusted me in a purchase or sale. If the lifetime value of a client in real estate is around $150,000, that is three million in lifetime earnings you can gain from one year of doing regular open houses. Of course, you won't meet every client on their first purchase, so these numbers are estimates, but it gives you an idea of what open houses can do for your business over time. I haven't done an open house now for seven years, and I still sell more than seventy-five homes per year because I connect regularly with my database, which was largely built from the open houses early in my career. No one told me any techniques for doing open houses, so I had to learn by trial and error. I want to pass on to you everything I learned so that you can build your business by being amazing at open houses.

Remember that open houses are a numbers game. The more open houses you do, the more buyers and sellers you will meet. Depending on where you live in North American and the skills you have at converting leads, the chance of you selling the house you are holding an open house in is between 1 and 3 percent. Only 1 to 3 percent of people who go through an open house actually buy that house. Sounds dismal, doesn't it? That number makes open houses seem like a terrible idea and a waste of time. But here's the truth: you are not in an open house to sell that house; you are in an open house to meet people and convert them into clients. Let's look at some very enlightening stats. 80 percent of sellers use the first realtor they meet, 71 percent of buyers use the first realtor they meet in person. Those numbers tell us that an open house is exactly where you want to be. I haven't been able to verify these stats that are often cited online, but in my opinion, even if they are off by 20 percent, they still point to the truth that open houses are the best place to meet people who are looking to either buy or sell and to convert them into clients.

If your goal is not to sell the house, but rather to meet potential new clients, you will be much better at open houses. You don't have to be a pushy salesperson trying to sell the home you are in; you can simply have fun and build relationships that hopefully will lead to future sales. So let's look at some techniques that will help you elevate your career by doing open houses.

First, you need to know about the people coming to your open house. Too many salespeople will come into my office after a weekend of open houses and say it was a waste of time. They tell me the only people who showed up were the neighbours coming to tell me how much better their house was than the open house. That realtor has just missed some great opportunities.

The first type of person who comes to an open house is the "nosy neighbour." I love this group of people! They show up and pick apart the house and tell you how much better their house is. When I was new, this person would frustrate me, but I came to realize something important: these neighbours became my greatest source of referrals in that area. The nosy neighbours live in that area because they like it, and they want their friends and family to live near them. If you do a lot of open houses in the same neighbourhood, the neighbours will get to know you and will start referring you because you are top of mind and know and love their neighbourhood as much as they do. Bottom line? Treat the nosy neighbours like gold. Ask them lots of questions about their homes because they will be proud to talk about them. The more questions you ask, the more important they will feel and before you know it, they will be inviting you over to see their home. Here are some great questions you can ask to get a conversation going:

- What are some things you love about living in this area?
- What upgrades have you done to your house?
- What makes your house unique compared to this house?
- Is there anything I should know about this neighbourhood?

Do you see how all of these questions are about them and their house and not about you trying to sell them anything? If you ask them these types of questions, it will quickly disarm them. They will see that you aren't a pushy salesperson, and this will help foster a new relationship. For years, during a slow time in the market, I did open houses seven days a week in the same neighbourhood. It seemed like the only people who would ever come were the neighbours, and over time I built a relationship with everyone in the neighbourhood. I've told you already that I looked much younger than my age, and during this time, the moms in the area took pity on me and started bringing me baked goods almost every day! After a couple of years, I was "the guy" in that area and almost every person who sold or moved into the area used me as the agent because of the relationships I had built with the neighbours. This group of people can become huge asset to your business, so treat them accordingly.

The next type of person who will come through an open house is the dreamer, the professional looker. They enjoy coming to open houses to get ideas for their own house. For them, it is a fun way to spend a Saturday afternoon. These people can also be great for your business. They are in lots of open houses and are on top of the trends. They will move more often that the average person and real estate is always on their mind. Can you see why it is important to treat these people well? These people are great to have as clients because their transaction volume will be high. So ask them lots of questions, because they are knowledgeable and will love talking about real estate. Ask things like:

- What is your favourite area of the city?
- What is your favourite type of house?
- What would you change about this house?
- What are some of your favourite house trends?
- What colour would you paint this house?
- What colour have you painted your own house?

Notice that once again, all these questions are about them. Your goal is to make them feel important and to begin to build a relationship with them. Don't try to tell them how great the house you are in is; that will only make you seem like a pushy salesperson, and you will lose their trust.

Another type of person who will come through your open house is the serious buyer or seller. They are ready, willing, and able to pull the trigger on buying a house. Often these people don't know exactly what they want, but they know they want to buy a home and are interviewing realtors and properties at the same time. These people have done the research, but don't have a strong relationship with a realtor yet, they are just waiting for the right house or the right realtor to show up. These clients come to open houses all the time without realtors ever knowing it, and it is important to know how to identify and work with these types of people. If they like you and the house you are in, they will likely use you to buy it or to buy another home and list their current one as an added bonus.

With this group of people, the same principle applies start with asking them questions. Never ask them if they are working with a realtor. They will often say yes because the question put them on their guard and their walls go up. They will think you are pushy and will not trust anything you say after that. Remember that your goal is always to build relationships. They will work with you if they like you, trust you, and if you can demonstrate your value. Here are some questions I have found very effective for building relationships with the serious buyer or seller:

- Are you from this area?
- What are you looking for in a house?
- What is most important to you in a house, the floor plan, price, or location?
- Are you looking for a certain school district?

These are broad questions at first that will help you get to know them. A technique I have often used is to book a viewing at another home in the area for one hour after the open house ends. That way, if you bump into a serious buyer or seller in your open house, you can offer to show them a comparable house right away! This demonstrates to them that you are hard-working and looking out for their best interest, and it will go a long way to building trust. The likelihood of converting these serious buyers or sellers into clients will be very high.

Now that we have identified the three main types of people coming to your open house, I want to give you six steps to running an effective open house.

Step 1:
Identify your target market. It is important to do open houses in the area that you want to focus on. If you want to sell high-end homes, then that is the type of house you want to target. You also need to be consistent in one area. Too many realtors move to a new area every weekend and wonder why they struggle to gain traction. My advice is to do open houses in the area where most of your database lives, and do open houses that line up with who you are. If you are a middle-class person living in the suburbs and most of your database lives in that area, then that is the market you should target. You will attract people who are like you.

Another factor when identifying your market is to make sure there is a high volume of sales in the target area. Avoid doing open houses in an area that isn't selling: go fishing where the fish are. For example, it can be very hard to sell expensive homes in a down market, while cheaper houses will still sell regardless of market conditions. Once you have identified your target market, choose an effective time for your open house. Throughout my career, I have found Saturday and Sunday from two to four to be the best time but have also had success with weekdays from four to six when people are getting home from work. Other realtors have had success hosting sunset open houses.

Step 2:
Advertise in advance. This is a simple but often overlooked principle. People need to know that an open house is happening, and it also provides a great method of secondary advertising for you. The more you advertise your open house, the more people will notice your name. On the day of the open house, you should

have as many directionals as possible and flags all over the property. Your goal is to make it impossible for anyone who lives anywhere near the open house not to see your signs. Remember that you want all the nosy neighbours to show up and see how hard you work, so they will know that if they use you as their realtor, you will work just as hard for them. You can also advertise your open house through social media, newspapers, radio, local MLS systems and so on. Something else I recommend is knocking on at least fifty doors in the neighbourhood to invite all the neighbours to your open house. In my experience, after one house is listed in a neighbourhood, another one will usually be listed within two weeks. If you find this person, you will have a chance at selling their home. Door-knocking with an invite shows you have a good work ethic and will get more people to the open house for you to begin building relationships with.

Step 3:
Be prepared. You must have the house ready and open at least ten minutes before the advertised time. If you are five minutes late and there is already a line-up of people at the door, it will make you look unprofessional and disorganized. You also need to dress properly. In today's world, I don't recommend a suit (unless you are in an upscale market), but I also don't recommend sweatpants and a hat. You should find a professional medium so that you are approachable yet classy. The house also needs to be ready. You should arrive early enough to have all the lights on, the blinds open, and the house at a comfortable temperature. You also need to be prepared with market knowledge. You should know every comparable property in the area and have feature sheets available if potential client asks. The more you know about the area, the more professional you will seem. It's even a good idea to have viewed some homes in advance so you know more about the area. Being prepared will help you

appear professional and knowledgeable and potential clients will see the value you will bring if they use you as their realtor.

Step 4:
How to welcome people to the open house. First impressions will set the tone for your ability to close any potential clients. Here is how I recommend greeting people when they walk into a house:

First, I always give them a little space when they walk in. Don't run to the front door and give them a crushing handshake and start telling them how awesome the house is. Let them open the door and start walking towards you. This is the moment when you need to read the room. If the potential client comes in and avoids eye contact with you and walks towards the first room, let them have their space so they can soften up. They will eventually come to you, so don't chase them. On the other hand, if the potential client comes in and makes eye contact with you, then feel free to walk up to them, say hello and shake their hand, introduce yourself and say you are available to answer any questions. At this point, I set the tone by telling them to feel at home and wander through the house at their leisure, I will be in the kitchen if they have any questions. This is strategic because the kitchen is usually the most popular part of the house, and I know they will want to come and see it. After they have toured the house and come back to the kitchen, it is your chance to start building relationships by asking great questions. You will already have built a level of trust with them because you weren't a pushy salesperson following them through the house.

When they eventually come to the kitchen, I always start with the question "are you from around here?" This is a nonthreatening question and will help you figure out the type of person you are talking to. Their answer will also determine what your next questions will be. If they are from out of town, you can ask them how well they know the area. If they are from the area, you can ask them why they like this particular neighbourhood. If they are neighbours, you can start asking them about their house. The goal is to start a conversation where you can learn as much as possible about them and demonstrate your local knowledge. If you feel like you have built some good rapport, then you can try and do a soft close. I do this with two questions. The first question I ask is if they would let me take them on a buyer education tour, where I show them four to six other properties so they can get to know the area better. I clarify that they are not allowed to buy a house, it is to educate them about the area so there are no strings attached to my offer. More often than not, people will say yes, and voilà! I have just done a soft close. The moment I meet with them in my car the next day is the moment I know I have new clients. If they are willing to go look at houses with you, then there is a very high chance they will trust you to be their realtor. The next soft close I do is to ask if they are pre-qualified for a mortgage and refer them to my mortgage broker to help them. If they use my mortgage broker, there is a good chance they will also use me to be their realtor. This is a much better tactic than asking if they have a realtor. If you ask that question, then expect them to say yes and put up walls because it was a pushy question, and you have just lost the chance to convert them into customers. I will talk in detail about core connections later, but they are people or businesses that you have a reciprocal arrangement with: you give them business and they refer business back to you. Through the questions you have asked the potential clients, you may learn that they want to paint their house before they list. You can then refer your painter to them. This will show the value you bring them and increase your chance of getting a call later. The more you can get potential clients working with your core connections, the higher the chance that they will call you to buy or sell in the future.

Step 5:

Value statements. This is the part of running an open house that really matters. People want to work with a high-producing realtor who is successful and hard-working. The trouble is you can't just tell people how great you are. It will come off poorly, and they won't believe you anyway. We all know the person who can't wait to tell you how amazing they are at something. Most of the time, we roll our eyes and try to find a way out of the conversation. We don't want to have this effect on the potential clients coming through our open houses! The goal is to tell them how great you are without telling them how great you are. We do this by using a value statement. The value statement is a flyer that contains what potential clients can expect when they work with you. It will include client testimonials, awards you have won, a brief biography, and what you have to offer them when they work with you. When a person is about to leave the open house, this is your chance to give them a package about the house and your value statement. A person might visit six open houses that day and meet six different realtors. If they enjoyed a conversation with you, got a referral to a great mortgage broker, and are able to read about everything you offer, the chances of converting them to a client is high. It's almost like speed dating, where you want to give as much information as you can in a short period of time, hoping to get a call later. The value statement is non-invasive and gives the potential clients time to research you and decide if they want to work with you. This is a powerful tool and should be used by every realtor at every open house.

Step 6:

Increasing productivity. Open houses should be viewed as your second office space, which increases productivity because you are doing two things at the same time. If you are sitting in your office, you have no chance of meeting new clients while you work, but in an open house, you can get work done and have a chance of meeting new people. This took me a few years to learn. At first, I would sit in an open house and play chess on my computer while waiting for potential clients to show up. I got really good at chess, but I wasted a lot of hours. Eventually, I realized this was valuable time to be working on my business. I started bringing books that I didn't have time to read, or I worked on my flyers, website, or database. Open houses became a place where I got a lot of work done with very little distraction. The time spent in an open house can be very valuable even if potential clients don't show up. Think of it as free office space every day for two hours when you can work on bringing your business to the next level.

Geographical Farming

Geographical farming means picking an area that you want to work in and trying to become known as the go-to real estate professional in that area. Geographical farming is the third largest source of generating new clients and should be a part of your business. When people go to buy or sell in that area, they will call you because they will see you as the expert. I have seen many realtors have as much as 50 percent market share in their farming area. Your farm area can be big or small depending on your resources of time and money. Most agents go too big too fast and fail over time. A geographical area can be as simple as a gated community, an apartment, small neighbourhood, or a townhouse site. The best part about geographically farming is how easy it is to do. If done correctly, farming should take less than three hours per week. It is a great way to increase new clients without a ton of effort.

How do you farm in real estate? The first thing you need to do is evaluate where you want to farm. What type of homes do you want to sell and what kind of client do you want to work with? If you are a middle-class person, then farm in a middle-class area. Just like open houses, you need to target your market. The next consideration is the absorption or turnover rate of the neighbourhood you are targeting. The goal is to farm an area where at least 12 percent of homes sell every year. That means twelve out of one hundred homes sell every year in that neighbourhood. There is no point farming an area if there is no turnover. So do the math in any area that you are considering. I also recommend targeting an area where first time buyers buy. I target these complexes because a first-time buyer is very valuable to a realtor's business. First time buyers will buy and sell for the longest period of time, and you have the opportunity to be their realtor for life.

Once you have picked an area, you need to commit to being consistent for at least two years. Farm areas can take a lot of time to grow, but once they are producing, it is a major source of business. Too many agents give up after six months or are inconsistent and then complain that their farm area doesn't work. If you are new, I would start small and target fifty to one hundred homes. If you are more experienced and have an assistant, then you can go much bigger.

What do I send to my farm area? This is the easiest part. Your farm area is just an extension of your database. If you mail something to your database twelve times a year, then do the same to your farm area. The only difference is that your market updates must be an update for that specific area, which is simple to do. Just take the one hundred homes in your area and give them the stats of how many homes have sold, what they sold for, and how many days they were on the market. You need to prove that you know everything about the area. Everything else you send will be the same things you send to your database.

The next goal of your farm area is to be visible everywhere. Target all your marketing and open houses there so your potential clients will see your face on a regular basis. You want to stay top of mind through billboards and bus benches, and you can even sponsor events in that area. Farming is simple and effective if you are strategic in picking your area and working it consistently.

Actively interacting with your SOI database, open houses, and geographical farming are three of the most effective methods of attracting new clients. I hope I have convinced you that "attraction" is a cost-effective and time-efficient way to generate new clients and a whole lot more fun than chasing them!

Chapter 4: Keep Clients

Systems of Contact

Keeping clients is the simplest part of the three-part equation to building a mature real estate business (get clients, keep clients, get referrals), yet few agents actually spend time on it. The stats are astounding. Ninety percent of buyers and sellers say they enjoyed their realtor and they would use them again, yet only 13 percent actually use the same realtor on the next transaction. When asked the reason why they didn't use their realtor again, the number one answer was that they forgot their realtor's name! This should embarrass us as an industry. Knowing this stat and making sure it never happens to you will give you a major advantage over the competition. Other realtors get stuck running on a hamster wheel day after day, chasing down new business instead of spending time investing in their old clients.

To build a mature business, you need to have a wide-open front door but a back door that is firmly closed. Repeat customers are the best to work with. They already know you, like you and trust you, and the cost to market to them is very low. If every realtor adopted a strategy to keep their existing clients, it would completely change their business. We would have wealthier agents with more manageable lives because they wouldn't be spending all their time chasing new business. I would argue that everything that gives realtors a bad reputation for being cheesy and pushy would disappear if more agents would invest time into keeping their clients. Lead companies would go broke, you would stop door-knocking, cold-calling, marketing, and even hosting open houses. Don't get me wrong, you do need to do these activities to build a database, but you do not need to continue doing them as your career advances. I know this because I have practiced it for the last eight years. For eight years, I have only focused on repeat clients and referrals and have not sold less than seventy-five homes per year. If I wanted to sell more homes, I could start doing open houses or marketing again, but there is no need. Seventy-five sales per year is a great work/life balance and provides a great income. Let's look at some practical ways that can help you get off the hamster wheel and close the back door to your business.

Regular Contact

Regular contact is the most important way to keep your existing clients. I am assuming you already displayed great customer service and competency during the transaction because 84 percent of clients say they were happy with their agent. So our goal is to get our clients to not only remember our name, but to be top of mind when they want to buy or sell the next time. Consistent contact is the only way to do this. This isn't rocket science, and there are some ways that work better than others, but what matters is that you have a plan! Unfortunately, this is where most agents fail: they have the best intentions to keep in contact, but they get busy and forget as time goes on. Then, when too much time has passed, the realtor is scared to contact their old client because it has been too long, and they don't know what to say. Intentions without a plan is a recipe for failure. We need to save ourselves from ourselves and build a plan and stick to it.

The plan needs to have two characteristics to be successful. You need to have a comprehensive database and you need to have a schedule of when and how they will be contacted. The goal for keeping clients is to have them as warm contacts at all times. A warm contact is someone you are in rhythm with. You are in regular contact, and the relationship has been maintained. Your client feels like you care about them and that you want to help. When you call a warm contact, the conversation doesn't feel awkward or forced, because you have talked to them recently. If you ever get a call from a client saying "Hey, I am Sally, do you remember me?" this means that you are failing to keep your database warm or even active. The call from Sally should sound like this: "Hey, thanks for the latest market update! How are your kids doing these days?" For your warm contacts, you are a trusted advisor in their life, and you will be the first call they make when they are thinking of buying or selling. So how do we stay in regular contact to keep our database warm?

The system that works the best is one that is consistent. You must be in contact with your database and past clients at least twelve times per year, and emails don't count. These touches must be of value to the client and build up the relationship. Your plan should have a healthy mix of different items that you send on a monthly basis. I went into great detail about this in Chapter 4, and I recommend going back and reviewing the different types of contacts you should be making with your database twelve times per year: market updates, personal connections, items of value, evidence of success, and drip email.

If your database and past clients get mail from you twelve times per year, it will be impossible for them to forget your name. It's easier than you think, and this will automatically separate you from most salespeople. This 12-point system is easy to set up and can be organized in the winter months when the market is slow. In the Pacific Northwest for example, December and January are slow months in real estate. You should take this time to write all your handwritten cards for the year and order all your swag and design all of your content. That way, when the spring market comes, you will not have to think about what to send because everything will be ready to go. The other thing to note it that this whole system can be easily set up and executed by an assistant. As your business grows, this is the perfect thing to hand off so you can leverage your time.

Lifetime Value of a Client

Never underestimate the value of a client over a lifetime. Too many realtors spend all their time chasing new leads and never consider retention. They have a huge front door for new clients to enter, but the back door is wide open because zero effort is spent on retention. Instead of focussing on repeat buyers and referrals, they chase the immediate. If realtors actually knew the lifetime value of a client, and invested their time here, their business would explode.

I estimate the average lifetime value of a client to be about $190,000. I arrived at this estimated number based off simple calculations. Currently the average commission is about $10,500 per transaction in my market. If you work with the same client and buy and sell four homes throughout your career, then you will receive $84,000.00 in commissions. On top of that you will most likely get at least a referral a year or every couple of years. Let's say you get a referral every second year for twenty years. That would end up being ten more transactions for a total of $105,000 in commissions. If you have twenty good clients, their lifetime value is $3.8 million dollars. We also need to be accurate and realistic with this number. Let's say the average person is only a buyer or seller for fifty years (they buy their first home at twenty-five and sell their last home at seventy-five), if you are in real estate for twenty-five years, it's safe to assume you can capture half of the lifetime value. That means that you will get $85,000 per client if you retain them. If you can get 150 people in your database, that would be an income of $12,750,000 over your twenty-five-year career. These are staggering numbers. If you set up your business to focus on turning new clients into lifetime clients, you will have a consistent and enjoyable business. You will never have to worry about the next sale or the length of your sales slump.

It was my sixth year in the business, and the market was still slow. I was still doing open houses seven days a week. One day, a young couple came into one of my open houses, and during our conversation, they told me that they owned a property that they couldn't sell, and they wanted to sell it so they could continue to renovate and flip homes. I met them at their house, and I ended up getting the listing. I sold their home, and then turned my focus to cultivating the relationship and staying connected with them, like I did with all my clients. Ten years later, they are some of my favourite clients and I have now sold over thirty properties with them.

It pays to stop chasing new clients and start playing the long game of cultivating lifetime relationships by providing great service and bringing value through consistent connection long after that first sale is completed.

Chapter 5: Get Referrals

Why do people refer realtors? Receiving a referral is the most rewarding part of our business because it is evidence that we are doing a great job. The more referrals you get, the more confidence you can have in your performance as a realtor. There is nothing better than a call from a past client saying that their sister is moving into town, and they would love you to help her find a house. Referrals are such an honour and should not be taken lightly. If someone refers you, it means they trust you enough to take care of their good friend or loved one, and they are confident you will not make them look bad. Getting referrals should be a major part of every realtor's business.

Your goal should be to have 33 percent of your business come from referrals. The concept of referrals is simpler than you think. I would argue that giving a referral is an emotional response that is backed up by logic. For example, if you really like a movie, you will refer it to your friends and family, right? The movie stirred an emotional response in you, but you will use logic to tell everyone why you liked it. You will tell people the acting was great, or the storyline was appealing, or the cinematography was awesome, but in reality, you are rationalizing the emotional feeling you experienced while watching that movie. The same thing happens in real estate. You will get referrals because of the emotional connection your clients had with you. When they enjoy this emotional connection, they will want to refer you. The emotional connection will be rationalized by your performance during the transaction, but the real reason they will refer you is because of the emotional connection.

In order to receive referrals, we need to focus first on building great connections and second on doing a great job to give our clients the logical reasons to refer us. This is why giving a financial incentive doesn't actually increase referrals for the most part, it's just a way for you to help people rationalize giving the referral. People will refer you because they know, like, and trust you. It's that simple.

How to Increase Referrals

Building an emotional connection in real estate can be hard to explain because it is an art, but it is also a skill that anyone can develop. When you feel connected to someone, you often explain it by saying that the other person just "gets" me. We don't know how to explain it, but we can feel it. We all have those people in our lives who "get" us. With these people, trust is high, conversations flow freely, and we feel a deep satisfaction with the relationship. The two parties seem to believe the best about each other. This is the type of relationship we want to build with our clients, regardless of whether or not they will refer us. If you are building a relationship for the sole purpose of a referral, people will see right through you. You need to be a person who believes in building great relationships for their own sake and referrals will come naturally.

The first way to build a great connection is through outstanding customer service. Emotional connections are built through giving, not taking. You need to be attentive and anticipate all the needs of your clients during the transaction. Little things matter. For every meeting, always show up with a coffee for your clients. Smile a lot and treat them kindly. Ask them how they are feeling a lot during the whole process. There have been many times when I can tell a client is uncomfortable with something, so I stop and ask how they are feeling. I want them to verbalize any emotions as quickly as possible. You want to be a safe person for your clients. If they are happy, sad, anxious, or angry, you want them to feel they can share that with you so ask them often how they are feeling. Remember the old saying "It's not what you say, it's how you say it"? In real estate, this means you don't have to say everything perfectly, but communicating that you care about your clients is what matters most.

Emotional connections are also built by giving people your time. When you are with your client, make sure you do not appear to be busy with other things. If you are constantly checking your phone or telling them how busy you are, they will shut down. Your clients need to feel important, so be careful to treat them that way. I have a little game I play with most people that they are unaware of. I pretend that they have a tattoo on their forehead that says MMFI. MMFI stands for Make Me Feel Important. Everyone wants to feel important, and my goal is to make my clients feel that way. When you give your clients your time and make them feel important, your emotional connection will grow. Whenever you are in-person with your clients, always focus on the human connection first, rather than the task. That is how all the best relationship builders approach life and so should we! When you are not in-person, you need to be very proactive to show that you care and have your clients' best interests at heart. You should be the one to discover any issues that come up during a transaction and bring them up as soon as possible. You should be on top of financing, home inspections, insurance, and any neighbourhood concerns before your clients become aware of them. The more proactive you are, the more your clients will trust you. The more problems you anticipate in advance, the better your relationship will be.

Systems to Implement that will Lead to more Referrals

When we have done a great job of building an emotional connection with our clients, they will want to refer us, we just need to help them get better at it. Our clients might know, like, and trust us, and they may want to refer us, but one problem always comes up: life gets busy, and they simply forget. There are some things that we can do to help our clients do a better job of referring us. Systems are the lifeblood of real estate and putting them to work for you will help you build a culture of referrals with your clients.

The first part of your referral system should be sending flyers out in the mail at least twice a year. The timing of these flyers is important. For most of North America, there are two busy real estate markets per year: the spring market and the fall market. The majority of the yearly sales happen in these two markets. If we know that buyers and sellers will be thinking of selling during a certain time, then we want to send out referral letters just before the spring market and just before the fall market, so that we are top of mind when they are discussing possible moves with their families and friends. The letter will usually have a cash incentive, so the people on your database have a way to rationalize referring you. They may refer you anyway, but if they recently received a letter reminding them that you will pay cash for a referral, the chance of being top of mind is much greater. You can't predict who will be buying and selling, but if three hundred people in your database run into a conversation with someone who wants to move, there is a good chance your name will come up. If the spring market starts in March, then the referral newsletter should go out in February. For the fall market that starts in September, the referral card should go out in August.

Part of your referral system should be to use surveys after every transaction. Our goal is to show our clients how important good service is to us and how much we appreciate referrals. This survey will help build your culture of referrals and it is easy to implement. All you have to do is create a survey that can be easily filled out and sent back to you. The best success for clients actually filling it out is a paper survey with the return address and a postage paid envelope along with it. This seems old school in today's online world, but in my experience, paper surveys have had the best results. The survey must have the basics about your service and how you can do better next time, but the really important part is the section about referrals. You will include a section that says: would you refer me in the future? Yes, or no? And a spot for testimonials. When you have this in your survey, you are communicating to your client that referrals matter to you and that you want them to refer you in the future. This survey should be given to your clients on closing day with whatever gift you give them.

Another part of your system is how you reward your referrals. It needs to be the same every time and done in a way that increases your chance of more referrals in the future. A reality is that family groups seem to move at the same time. If a sister moves, her brother and parents will likely move within a year. It's seems like it can't be true, but I have noticed it many times in my career. What this means to you is that when people are moving, they will be talking to all their friends and family about their move, which in turn makes everyone they talk to about it wants to move too. So you want to stay top of mind for as long as possible in order for those conversations to turn into referrals for their friends and family members to use you as their realtor.

One way to stay top of mind for a long period of time is to send a hand-written card with a small gift card (like ten dollars to Starbucks) when a client gives you a referral. My card will say something like this: *Susan, thanks so much for the referral of your sister Sally. I look forward to working with her and her husband, and I will take great care of them. Referrals mean a lot to me, so I wanted to say thanks. When the sale closes, I will send you $350 cash. Thanks again.* This is easy to do and only takes five minutes. This little note will build a culture of referrals because the referee will be excited to get the cash when everything completes. We know completion might be two to five months away and now we have a past client who has us on their mind because they are looking forward to getting some money in a few months. You will be top of mind during the whole transaction and increase your chances of another referral. It's also a kind thing to do and should be done anyway! The last aspect of rewarding a referee is keeping the referee updated throughout the transaction. This shows how much you care and proves you are doing a great job of taking care of the person who was referred to you. You should send a simple text message or a quick phone call three or four times during the process to say something like: *Hey John, just keeping you updated on your sister Susan. We looked at six homes today, none of them seemed to fit, but I am confident we will find a great home soon. Thanks again for the referral and enjoy your day.* Little messages like this will make a huge difference to your career as you build an amazing culture of referrals with your clients.

When you build a culture of referrals, your business will become easy. You will sell more homes in less time and make more money. Transactions will become less stressful because you will have trust at the foundation right from the start and everyone will enjoy the process. As your business matures, referrals should be high on your target list. Remember by year five in the business, 33 percent of your sales should be coming from referrals.

Chapter 6: Be the Best Version of Yourself

I heard a quote a while ago and it really impacted me: "Lazy people do a little work and think they should be winning; winners work as hard as possible and still worry if they are being lazy." Real estate can be brutal. We work long hours under incredible amounts of stress. It's easy to lose control of our time to keep our clients happy. When a client wants to see a house or write an offer, we drop everything to make it happen. So when the day is done and the client got the house they wanted, what about you? My guess is that you stuffed your face with fast-food on the way to the meeting, got home after your kids were in bed, and finished the night with a few glasses of wine to calm the nerves. This is a familiar story for many realtors. But what happens when this sort of day becomes every day? We suffer and so do our loved ones.

The stats are scary. Five percent of realtors are alcoholics, the divorce rate is higher than average, and many realtors have lost control of their time and their health. Many agents I know are burnt out, obese, and some have suffered from early heart attacks. Several years ago, I was sitting in my doctor's office thinking I was dying of a brain tumor or at the very least having a heart attack. I couldn't sleep. I would wake up sweating, and my heart was racing and skipping a beat every few beats. What was worse, I would wake up exhausted in the morning with a pressure in my head that was so intense I wanted to drill a hole in my skull to relieve it. To top it off, I had constant diarrhea. Sorry for the TMI (too much information) but that is where my health was at. The doctor told me that I was only thirty, so the chances of a heart attack, brain tumor, or colon cancer were very, very low. I still wasn't convinced. I had spent several hours with Dr. Google and was ready to buy my casket and plan my funeral. My doctor ran all of the necessary tests, and they all came back negative. Then he asked me about the stress in my life. My immediate response was that I didn't have very much stress in my life, but it got me thinking.

I went to a naturopath next. I paid for all the blood tests and followed all of their instructions. They thought I might have allergies, so I cut out booze, corn, gluten, and everything else that tasted good. It didn't make any difference. I spent a whole summer without a cold beer or a cob of corn, and I still had no answer for why I felt so terrible. The naturopath started asking me about my lifestyle and stress levels and emphasized the importance of a healthy and balanced life. I told her I didn't feel stressed, so that couldn't be it. She then started talking about how important it was to sleep well, eat right, and get lots of exercise. That got my attention, so I slowed down and listened. Was I sleeping eight hours a night? No. Was I exercising regularly? No. Was I eating clean? Not even close. Was I taking time for meditation or spirituality? No. My answer was no to everything she asked.

A week later, one of my colleagues called me "puffy." I was so delusional at this point that I got offended instead of thinking that maybe he was right. To top it off, he asked if I was ever winded after walking up the stairs. Those two comments ran around in my head for a few weeks before I thought that maybe my life was out of control. Maybe I was giving everything I had to other people and the person paying the biggest price was me. I was a "yes" person and every time I said yes to someone else, I was saying no to me. After doing a review of my current lifestyle, I realized that I was saying no to me at the expense of my health.

In theory, our clients want us to enjoy family, free time, and pursue health and fitness until the moment they want to know something about their house listing. A client does not do well when you say, "Sorry I didn't respond for four hours because I was on a hike on a Wednesday afternoon" or "I was taking a lunch break." They don't want to hear that you don't work on Sundays or don't respond to calls or texts after 8:00 p.m. because it is family time. In the end, whose fault is it if you lose your family or your health suffers? The only person you have to blame is yourself.

Our clients need clear boundaries, and you need to prioritize yourself, your family, and your health. When you can operate as the best possible version of yourself, your clients win anyway! Everyone has heard the story of the two men chopping wood. Here is the version I remember: Two men had one week to chop a certain amount of wood each. One man was big and strong and was willing to put in long hours. The other man was smaller and did not have the physique of a lumberjack. On day one, the big man worked all day chopping wood while the smaller one spent the day sharpening and honing his axe. At the end of day one, the big man was ahead. When day two started, the big man was back swinging hard and sweating as his axe was getting duller and duller, but instead of being concerned, he simply swung harder.

The smaller man took his sharpened axe and began making precise and strategic swings. His every move had a purpose. He even quit a few hours earlier than the big man, to spend some more time sharpening his axe. At the end of day two, the big man was still ahead. When day three started, the big man had blisters and hadn't slept because his muscles were sore, but he pushed through and swung all the harder. He pushed all day and didn't even take a break. He hurled insults like "water is for the weak" and "rest is for the soft," but on the inside, he could tell that the smaller man was catching up. Day four came and the tables had turned. The smaller guy's pile of wood was bigger, and he seemed relaxed and in control. His axe was sharp, and he was fresh. He wasn't concerned about his competition because he was being the best version of himself. At this point, the bigger guy was taking five swings to the small guy's one because his axe was so dull. Trying to catch up, he worked through the night and into day five. Day five came and the smaller man had a pile twice the size of the bigger man. He finished with a sharp axe and was ready for the next week. In contrast, the big man was burned out, angry, and jealous that he had only cut half the amount of wood the smaller guy had.

You and I can learn a valuable lesson from this. We must be the best version of ourselves before we can serve others. I have learned this the hard way, and I have a feeling that many of you have been there too. If you haven't, I hope you will heed this warning and make the changes necessary to your life so that you can become the best version of yourself.

Healthy Body Healthy Mind

If we want to be the best version of ourselves, we need a healthy body. This manifests itself in two ways. How you move and what you eat. Have you ever noticed that some of the highest achievers in the business world are also extremely fit? How can this be? They have the least time and the most stress, yet they run marathons, go hiking, and are clearly physically fit. Successful people know how important a healthy body is for a productive lifestyle. Most people, if left to their own ways, will not exercise, or eat well. I am the worst at this. No one loves nachos and apple fritters more than me. I am also a sucker for fast-food and binge eating after 8:00 p.m. And for me, the more stressful my life is, the more and the worse I eat! Real estate agents struggle with this more than those in other industries. We have good intentions when we bring healthy leftovers from home that require a fork, knife, microwave, and twenty minutes of peace to eat, but suddenly it is 2:00 p.m., your next meeting is at 2:15 p.m., and it's just easier to hit the drive-through. No forks or knives required! Some realtors also seem to think that part of our job is going for lunch every day. Meeting clients and drinking beer seems to be a way to network. Unfortunately, this is expensive, a major time suck, and the calories add up fast. Not to mention that when you are full of bad food and booze, I promise you will be less productive for the rest of the day.

Like everything else, you need to have a plan for your eating habits if you are going to do it right. Stock the locations you work from with healthy foods. Your office and car should have water, healthy snacks, and a healthy, easy-to-eat lunch. You need to learn what foods fuel your body the best and create a weekly plan. Currently, I bring two apples and a muffin with me for snacks every day, and I order healthy, ready-to-eat meals from a fitness guru that are always in our office fridge waiting for me.

Consistent exercise is also really important. This has become a habit in my life, and now I feel terrible if I don't exercise for a few days. Exercise can take many forms and happen at any time of the day, but this is what I know: if you don't have a plan, exercise will be the first thing you sacrifice when the day gets rolling. Good intentions are not a plan, so if you don't plan exercise into your day, it will not happen. My favourite time and type of exercise has changed throughout the different stages of my career. I have tried almost every time of the day and have found pros and cons to all of them. Through trial and error, I have found that my favourite time to exercise is on my way home at the end of the day. There is nothing better than going for a run in the forest after a busy day. It gives me time to recap the day in my mind and enjoy God's creation. The more miles I run, the more I shed the stress of the day. It's a great way to reset my body and have a fresh mindset for my family. This is also the most difficult time for real estate agents as many clients want to see houses in the afternoon, so you might have to choose a different time of the day. The point is that there is no perfect time, as long as you exercise three to five times a week. I find it much easier to stay consistent and to push myself when I set health goals for myself. My goals have ranged from running marathons, to playing squash, to working towards a better physique. It doesn't matter what it is, as long as you have a plan to make exercise a part of your routine until it becomes a habit.

Mindset / Grit

Mindset is everything. I believe that people who have less than average talent or ability can compete with the most talented people in the world because mindset and determination are the great equalizers. We see this in play all around us, but it is the most evident in sports. The greatest athletes are not the most talented ones, they are the ones who have the highest level of work ethic, determination, and desire to win. In any field, the most successful people are the ones who put in the most effort behind the scenes. They are working when others aren't. You will see them working in the non-sexy moments when no one is watching. They quietly get to work early and are back at it after their kids have gone to bed. If you have a resolute mindset and strong work ethic, anything is possible.

A few years ago, a new agent joined our office. He was nineteen and had battled and beat leukemia when he was in high school. We were hanging out one night and came up with the idea to run 103 km (from the city we lived into our region's Children's Hospital) to raise $100,000 for cancer research. We wanted to make the run ten months from the time we came up with the idea. When I woke up the next morning, I was panicked. I had never run more than 15 km at one time in my life! Plus, I was in my late thirties and over 200 lbs. One thing I knew I had though, was mindset. We started training in January in the freezing cold. Day by day we got stronger and faster. Soon we were running five days per week, and I completed my first ever marathon in May. The training schedule was gruelling. By that summer, a typical week of training looked like this: Monday 8 km, Tuesday 16 km, Wednesday 10 km and Friday 50 km. We were running 60 km to 80 km per week. We ran in snow, rain, heat, and everything in-between. We had to manage sore knees, blisters, and toenails falling off on the longer runs. There was no one cheering us on as we ground it out day after day after day, pushing ourselves beyond the limit of what we thought was possible.

At midnight on a cold night in October, we started our run. It's a moment I will never forget. There were at least one hundred people at the starting line to cheer us on and before we started, we were able to announce that not only had we reached the fundraising goal of $100,000 but we had surpassed it by $25,000 dollars. For the first 10 km, we had a group of people running with us and a convoy of vehicles. It was exhilarating and the energy of all these people made me feel like I could run forever. This reminds me of our real estate journey. The start is easy because we have this fresh energy and there hasn't been any adversity yet: it is just you and the goals you have set of where you want to be. But this feeling doesn't last, does it?

By 1:00 a.m. the group of runners had gone home, and only one car remained in the convoy along with some people on bikes for support. We still had 93 km left to run. The feeling of exhilaration was gone and before us was a long, cold, lonely journey. My body didn't hurt yet, but there was a battle raging in my mind. My mind was throwing accusations at me: *You can't do this, you're not good enough, you are too heavy, your knees will never last, you are going to let a lot of people down who donated money to this cause.* By 2:00 a.m. we had run a half marathon and that's when my body started to hurt.

The journey in this business is so similar. Before you know it, the excitement has worn off and the reality of the work sets in. Your brain is hardwired to want comfort, so it starts throwing those same accusations at you. You aren't good enough, you don't have good enough people skills, you have too many things on your plate, you should do something safer, you are a fraud. You also might find that well-meaning people in your life start to drag you down, too. You will hear things like, your life is out of balance, what is your end goal, you should get a real job, and the list goes on. When I started out, I even had people close to me tell me that I would likely fail. When I started a brokerage, someone tricked me by saying they wanted to take me for lunch. I thought they were going to congratulate or encourage me, but instead they spent an hour telling me all the ways I was going to fail. I want you to hear something very clearly: if the people in your life and the voices in your own head are throwing these accusations at you, you are probably on the right track. Obviously, we need to be humble, careful, and responsible, but I want you to know that you need the mindset to be able to weather this negativity and keep going through the storms of this real estate journey. If you want a long and successful career, you need the mindset to get you through the ups and downs.

We kept running through the night. I remember when we had reached the first marathon distance, the car riding with us hit the horn in farewell. It was bittersweet. One marathon down and one and a half to go and we were all alone. To be truthful, at that moment, I felt like there was no way I was going to make it, but I looked over at my friend and he was locked in and focused. If he was going to keep going, then I had to, too! I am incredibly proud of him as a person, and I needed his influence that night.

The night rolled on and we kept running. We were chasing the sunrise and couldn't wait to feel the warmth of a new day. I needed a boost as I was getting low on energy, and I was starting to get a weird pain on the outside of my left knee. Through the last ten months of training, I did not have this problem, so I assumed it would go away. I pushed through the pain and focussed only on the rising sun. At kilometer sixty, the sun started to rise and what a feeling it was! The cold dark night was over, and we were over halfway there. We stopped at kilometer sixty for a snack and some water and I knew I was in trouble. My knee felt like a rusty old joint that needed oil. After the break, I tried to run again, and I couldn't. All the training I had endured over the last ten months led to this moment, and my leg was betraying me. I felt like such a failure!

But when I looked over at my friend, I knew I wouldn't fail him. Maybe I couldn't run anymore, but I was going to support him every minute until he crossed the finish line. I swallowed my pride and got on a bicycle and followed him for the next thirty-three kilometers. Step after step he kept on going, his mental strength was so inspiring. At kilometer ninety-three, I had to try running again no matter the cost. I took pain medication and rubbed an icy cold ointment on my leg. We hobbled through the last 10 km together. Near the end, I could barely lift my feet to get over the speed bumps as we came up to the Children's Hospital. We were at the end of our journey, and I'm not ashamed to say that I started to cry. For the final leg, the hospital had put up pictures of the children currently in the hospital fighting for their lives, and suddenly it felt so insignificant to be worried about my knee. My friend and I were both crying now as we hobbled to the finish line with a huge crowd of our loved ones waiting for us. We looked up and the kids were at their hospital room windows holding up signs with my friend's name on them. He had been inside one of those rooms fighting for his own life only four years earlier. We found out later from one of the nurses that one of the little boys was running laps in his room so that when he got better, he could be just like us.

What a powerful, humbling, and heartbreaking moment this was for me. It taught me so many lessons that I have applied to my real estate journey and to my life. I hope that you can take some of the lessons I learned and apply them to your own journey. There is no limit to what you can accomplish with the right mindset and the determination to never give up.

Time Management

The ability to manage your time is incredibly important in the real estate industry. If you want to elevate your business and live a life of adventure and success, you must master your time efficiency. We are all given the exact same amount of time every day, so why do some people accomplish so much more than others with that time? How does Elon Musk run X (formerly Twitter), design spaceships, and build electric cars when some realtors don't think they have the time to sell twenty homes per year? Some of the most successful people I know exercise every day, eat healthy, and spend time with their loved ones. There is an art to time management, and I want to give you some sound tips that have worked for me over the years.

For more than a decade, I have sold an average of seventy-five homes per year on my own, I have built a real estate company to one hundred and twenty agents and $1 billion in sales, I own twenty rental doors, build an average of six homes per year, and do land development in-between. I also take at least ten weeks of vacations every year, I don't work Sundays, and most days I am home by 5:00 p.m. I am no different than you, so if I can do it, so can you!

We are going to dive into leverage, time blocking, and a few other tricks to help you learn how to better manage your time.

It's never been easier to waste time than it is today. There are thousands of the world's smartest people working for tech companies with the sole purpose of catching your attention and keeping it. These are the daily 2022 averages of how much time a person spends on each social media platform: TikTok 53 minutes, YouTube 47.8 minutes, Twitter 34 minutes, Snapchat 30 minutes, Facebook 30 minutes, and Instagram 33 minutes. These are scary numbers, especially since most people have all of those apps on their phones. The average person in North America also spends three hours watching TV per day. If we don't pay attention to where our time is spent, then the odds are definitely stacked against us.

In real estate, no one is looking over your shoulder telling you what to do. At any other job, your boss will notice immediately if you are wasting your time and not working hard. For example, my wife used to work for an accounting firm where every employee had to monitor their time every six minutes. Imagine if realtors evaluated what they did every six minutes. Many realtors say they work eight hours per day, but if they were honest, a lot of that time is wasted. I have had realtors sit in my office and tell me that their sales production isn't lining up with the time they are investing. When I ask them if they are doing core tasks like connecting with their database or other productive activities, I often get the excuse that they don't have enough time. At this point, I always do the same thing: I ask to see their phones to check on their social media apps for time spent every day. Inevitably, their faces go red, and more often than not they won't give me their phone because they know the truth. This may sound harsh, but my hope is that they will walk out of my office knowing they need to get their time management under control.

If you want to be productive, successful, and make a difference in this world, you need to find a way to take back your time. The truth is that you *do* have the time. You have all the time you need to be productive and successful. People often ask me how I manage to get so much done in a day. The simplest answer is that I am ruthless with my time, and I leverage as much as I can because I want to prioritize what matters. Here are some ways I have learned to take control of my time.

The first tip is to learn the art of time blocking. You should time block as many things in your life as possible to help you focus on time management. Anything that isn't time blocked in my calendar won't get done. For years, I wanted to go to the gym consistently, but I didn't time block it. I would tell myself that I would go to the gym when I had a window that day. Guess what happened? I never went to the gym. I realized that I had to save myself from myself, so I hired a personal trainer and time blocked the same time three days a week. After that, I never missed the gym again.

In real estate, some activities are harder to do than others, like connecting with people every single day. Prospecting is an activity that will not get done if it's not time blocked. Even five phone calls a day can make a huge difference in your sales numbers at the end of the year. This is something you must prioritize; therefore, it must be time blocked.

The next tip to improve your time management is the ability to leverage your time. Years ago, I hit a wall at forty sales per year, even though it seemed like I was working every waking hour. So I set out to learn new ways to be efficient with my time, and I want to share them with you.

If you are worth one hundred dollars per hour selling real estate, then you should not be doing tasks that can be done for twenty dollars an hour. Here's what I want you to do: write down every task that you perform for two weeks, even the small things like checking your email, replying to clients, writing cards, it all goes on the list. Then take another piece of paper and put a line down the middle. On one side write down the jobs that are worth the most per hour (the jobs only you can do), and on the other side all of the tasks that can be performed by someone else. This list of items will be different for everyone, but regardless, you will soon see that hiring an assistant for twenty dollars an hour will save you time and increase your efficiency. Tasks like paperwork, booking showings, photos, signs, lockboxes, and mail-outs, can all be done by an assistant for twenty dollars per hour. You should be doing the high dollar value activities like being face to face with buyers and sellers, and hiring an assistant will free up more of your time for these money-making activities. Another way to look at it is that with an assistant, you will get sixteen hours of work done in an eight-hour workday. You may not be able to afford a full-time assistant right away but as your business grows, you will be able to leverage more and more of your time. .

Time management also requires the ability to say no. I have struggled with this for most of my life, so I feel like a hypocrite giving you this advice. The more you succeed, the more people will expect that you should say yes to everything they ask. It makes sense because you will be personable, top of mind, and a person of influence, so you will be invited to golf tournaments, charity events, boards, awards galas, and the list goes on and on. In the moment it will be hard to say no, but you need to.

Whatever you say yes to means you are saying no to something else. If you say yes to an evening committee then you are saying no to putting your child to bed at night and reading them a story. If you say yes to volunteering on a Saturday morning, you are saying no to a hike that day. I think you can see the point. If you say yes to everything, you will resent the events and the people who invite you to them, and you will end up burned out. For the last few years, I have started saying no to almost everything and it feels so good. I value time with my family and adventure. When I started saying no to things, my time freed up so I could spend my time on the things I valued.

The last tip on time management is to do a time log every once and a while. This is simply evaluating your day, every day for a week to see where you spent your time. Check all of your phone apps every day and add up the time, write down how long you watched TV or how much time you spent chatting with co-workers. This might sound extreme, but I promise it will make a difference. We are all human and bad habits tend to creep in without us realizing. Many personal trainers will ask you to do a food log so you can see how the wrong food or too much food will stop you from reaching your fitness goals. What the wrong food is to fitness, time wasting is to the business world. So do a refresh every so often and take an honest look at where your time is spent. The goal is to be in control of your life and not a slave to the people who design addictive apps. If you want to spend ten minutes a day on TikTok, that is great! Just set a timer so you follow through and your time doesn't slip away. If you have trouble sticking to time limits on certain platforms, delete that platform. You need to take back your time.

Sleeping Right

We all know that people need at least seven to nine hours of sleep every night, but how many people actually get that? Studies state that we need precisely eight hours and ten minutes to avoid detrimental function during our awake hours. The average North American adult sleeps 6.8 hours a night. Depression and obesity are now linked to sleep deprivation. Clearly, it is important to prioritize your sleep!

When I was at my worst point, I remember being completely mentally exhausted. I was selling over eighty homes per year by myself. The lights would be turned off by 10:30 p.m. but that did not mean my brain turned off. In fact, it almost seemed like turning the lights off turned my brain on! I would stress about what didn't get done that day or what needed to be done tomorrow. Or I would win fake arguments in my head from the injustices of the day or the week before. By 1:00 a.m. I would begin stressing that my alarm would be going off in five short hours. It was terrible.

What I learned was that just giving myself an eight-hour window for sleep wasn't enough. There were other habits in my life that needed to change before I would be able to actually sleep during that window. Here are some tips that really helped me. First of all, stop feeling the need to prove that you need less sleep than the average person. There is no badge of honor if you sleep less than your friends and still manage to function. Next, get regular exercise every day, cut back on alcohol, and stay off your phone before bed. Pretend your phone is poison after 8:00 p.m. Your clients will ask you questions and demand your time at all hours. If you answer your phone at 9:00 p.m. once, your clients will always expect you to be available at that time. Being on your phone stops your brain from being able to wind down and get ready for sleep. This includes being on social media! At 10:00 p.m. right before you turn off the light, you will see that your competition has sold a house and you will wonder why you haven't, and then you will see that a friend has listed with a different agent and your brain goes into overdrive, and you have just self-sabotaged a good night's sleep.

Mindset of Learning

One of the core values in my office and for the people I teach is to always be learning. In my opinion, being willing to learn is truly a superpower. In my second year of real estate, I was frustrated, broke, and if I was honest with myself, failing at building a solid business. It is not an exaggeration to say that if I had let my ego get in the way at that point, I would have failed for sure. But instead, I made a decision that saved my career. I told you the story already, but the decision to ask my boss for help and then listening to the CD he gave me kickstarted my desire to learn from everyone and everything! This was my light bulb moment: if I wanted to be the best at my craft, it was time to start learning!

A whole world opened to me that I didn't even know existed. I read as many books as I could. On sales, closing, investing, leadership, psychology, and all the classics in-between. It seemed that the more I learned and the more I applied what I learned, the easier sales became. My career began to accelerate quickly, and sales became a fun challenge for me. I stopped comparing myself to the people around me because I had a new set of aspirations. I was able to raise my own bar and set and achieve goals that I never thought possible. If you have an attitude of learning and are willing to apply what you have learned, you will be unstoppable. I have no doubt that the biggest determiner of success is an attitude of learning. People who prioritize learning do not complain when things don't go their way, they simply evaluate their situation and find a way to improve. Developing a mindset of learning can change your situation for the better no matter what you are struggling with. So pick up a book and begin your learning journey. Don't be a victim of your circumstances, learn how to overcome them!

Surround Yourself with the Right People

If you want to be successful, you need to learn from people. Much of my success is because of the incredible people I have surrounded myself with. It is amazing what you can absorb through osmosis, just hanging around with amazing people. I have heard it said that we become the average of the five people we hang out with the most. If you want to be fit, get some fit friends. If you want to be a loving family person, spend time with people who love their spouse and care deeply about their kids. If you want to be wealthy, then hang out with some people who have achieved wealth without sacrificing everything else. If you want to be a great realtor, spend time with realtors you want to be like.

When deciding what real estate company to join, realtors ask about fees, tech, and a host of other things, but most of them never consider the leader of the company or the type of agents who work there. Your number one consideration should be the people who work in that company. Focus on finding a group of agents who you admire for living successful, well-balanced lives.

Another way to make this point is this: tell me who your friends are, and I will tell you who you will become. This can be tricky in real estate because many salespeople are not what they seem. I have met lots of realtors who sell over fifty properties a year and yet are broke, exhausted, and slaves to their work. If your only goal is to sell fifty properties per year, then maybe you want to learn from this person, but the purpose of this book is that you would sell fifty properties per year while enjoying what you do and living a healthy balanced life.

In order to find the right people to surround yourself with, you first have to define your own vision for your life. What do you want it to look like? What are your goals for your professional and personal life? These will be different for everyone, so make sure you stay true to who you are. After you've done this, you can start finding people who line up with your vision. At this point, many people get confused about what to do next. It seems weird to call someone out of the blue and say you want to be their friend or have them as a mentor, and I agree, that is weird, so please don't do that! What I want you to do once you've identified people who are living out the goals you have set for your own life, is to call them up and tell them you are impressed with them and would love to hear their story. Then ask them if they have time for a coffee or lunch. In my experience, most people will say yes to this request.

When you meet with them, there are a few rules to keep in mind. Rule number one is to pay for the lunch or coffee. Remember, these are usually successful people who are taking time out of their busy day to meet with you, so show your gratitude. The second rule is to ask questions. This will show them that you respect their time, and it is the best way to learn as much from them as possible. I love hearing people's stories, so I usually start with questions like, "Tell me why you and your wife have such a great marriage" or "Tell me how you became so successful in your business." Try to get them to start at the beginning. North America is made up of immigrants, and I love to know if they were born here and if their parents immigrated. It might seem like a funny question to ask, but it's a part of their story and it helps paint the picture of how they became the person they are today. Another great question is to ask them what they wanted to be when they were in high school because most entrepreneurs probably didn't think they would end up where they were during their years in school. This always gets a great conversation going.

When you surround yourself with people you want to be like, your world will change. I once read a book on finances and loved every minute of it. The book was sincere, to the point, and had sound advice that could be applied to everyone. I liked the book so much, I thought to myself that I would love to get to know the author. So I reached out to him and told him how much I enjoyed his book and asked if I could take him for lunch and he agreed! That's how easy it is to meet new people and start a relationship. One of my favourite people is a very savvy investor. He owns a lot of apartment buildings and hundreds of individual units. When I take him for lunch, he always asks when I am going to start buying or building apartments, like it's no big deal at all. He talks as if anyone can do what he's done, and he makes me less afraid of the risks. I am so glad he is a mentor in my life because he helps me believe that anything is possible. If my only friends were guys I hung out with in high school, still living in their parents' basements, would I even consider buying or building apartments? Many of my friends are in my life because I admire them and want to be like them. They are selfless, hardworking, caring, and incredible humans. I know that if I hang out with them, I will become a better version of myself over time.

Every salesperson should also hire a coach. The internet is a great platform to learn from people anywhere in the world. Online coaching makes finding a good coach easier than ever before. If you want to sell one hundred homes per year, then find a coach who has done it or helped other agents get there. If you want a coach to increase your wealth, then ask them how much they are worth before you sign up with them. Don't be afraid to ask hard questions and be as direct as possible. Finding a great coach is a strategic way to surround yourself with the right people, but make sure you hire someone who has achieved in the area you want to grow in.

The last part of surrounding yourself with the right people is giving back. To be the best versions of ourselves, we should be mentoring someone as well as being mentored. Having someone above you and below you is a healthy way to live. So make it a goal to reach out to the next generation and lend them a helping hand. There are few things in life as satisfying as helping someone reach their goals.

The Art of Consistency: Make Every Day Count

Every single one of us has the gifts, skills, and ability to have the life we desire. I firmly believe this! You are capable of more than you think, and I want to help you get there. If you consistently make every day count, you will achieve beyond your wildest dreams. This is true in real estate and true for every other part of life. If you take one small step forward every single day, you will look back in a year and be blown away with how far you have come.

Make Every Day Count (MEDC) has helped me achieve my goals more than almost any other principle. I am an average person who has been able to achieve at extraordinary levels because I have consistently made every day count. You can do the same. Consistency is a superpower we all possess; we just need to put it into action. Consistency will help you compete with the most talented people in any given field, including real estate. If you are like I used to be, you likely think success is for someone else. That is simply a lie that you tell yourself. We look up to these incredible people and think that we could be extraordinary too if only we were more like them. But guess what? Those people are just like you or me. It's true that some people have better connections, status, or talents, but that doesn't guarantee success. Society is full of talented people who blame circumstances or other people for them not achieving what they want. It is true that bad things sometimes happen that are totally outside of our control, and your bad things might be worse than my bad things, but I bet there are people who are worse off than both of us. So if we subscribe to the victim mentality, where does that leave us? Feeling sorry for ourselves, blaming others, and living a life of "shoulda' woulda' coulda's." Wouldn't you rather be able to tell people that despite the bad things that happened to you, you made the best of a terrible situation and changed your life? And then you can reach out to help others who have gone through something similar. With this attitude instead of the victim mentality, you will be a difference maker in this world. Making every day count will get you through hard times and help you accomplish anything you want to.

I know that "consistency" is not a sexy word, but it is the backbone to success in real estate. Almost all the struggling agents I talk to lack consistency in their business. Consistency affects every single part of your craft.

Let's look at some practical ways to add consistency to your business and make every day count.

First, you need to be at the office at the same time every day. You need to treat it like any other job. This can be your home office, but I strongly recommend that you work at your company office. Agents who work in the office are much more productive than agents who work from home. When you are at work, your brain knows you are at work and that's where your focus will be, and sales takes a lot of focus. If you are at home, you might have pets, or family members around who will distract you. You'll be sitting at your kitchen table looking around at the dishes that need to be washed or out the window at the lawn that needs to be mowed. It is hard for our brains to be in work mode when we are at home, and we need to set ourselves up for success.

I am at the office by 7:40 a.m. five days a week. I need a full hour to be able to prepare for the day that starts at 9:00 a.m. At 9:00 a.m. my phone starts ringing, and I want to be ready. In my preparation time before 9:00 a.m. I write a list of everything I want to accomplish for that day. I also go through my emails, phone messages, and any other communication apps to make sure I haven't missed anything from the previous day. The next thing I do is review my hot list. My hot list is comprised of any buyers or sellers who I expect to be buying a home in the next thirty to ninety days. These clients need to be followed up with often if you want to provide good service and get referrals. If you don't follow up a lot, you are also at risk of having them work with another salesperson who is better at follow up. The last thing I do during this time is make sure that all my meetings are lined up properly. To date, I communicate with a minimum of fifty different people every day. This translates to forty phone calls, one hundred emails, and three hundred text messages per day. If you aren't on the ball, it's easy to get lost with that volume of communication. But five days a week, I have my communications all done by 9:00 a.m. This hour of quiet before the day starts is the number one reason for my success because it allows me to spend the rest of the day working directly with people, and we all know that the more people we work with, the more homes we will sell. Unfortunately, many agents roll into the office at 10:00 a.m. with a coffee in hand. They then spend some time walking around the office socializing. By the time they start working, it is 11:00 a.m. and they are soon off to lunch (usually with another salesperson) for an hour and a half, and by then it's well into the afternoon. With this schedule, it is no wonder they don't succeed. Treat your business like any other job. Pretend you have a boss (who would fire you if you kept the hours I just described above). A good framework is to spend the first two to four hours in the office and the next four to six out in the world with clients or potential clients.

The art of consistency needs to also be in play with your database, open houses, marketing, and every other area of your business. Specific strategies for each of these areas have been discussed at length already in Chapter 4. The point I want to drive home here is that whatever structures and strategies you put into place in any area of your business, do them consistently! Aristotle had this figured out. An author named Will Durant summarized his idea in this quote: "We are what we repeatedly do. Excellence, then, is not an act, but a habit." The more habits you form, the easier sales will become, and you will see your business grow.

Chapter 7: Know Your Craft—Sales Skills

It was 2008 and the housing crash was in full swing. The year before, as a new agent, I had done over thirty transactions, but now I couldn't sell a house. Did I have sales skills? Back then I would have said a resounding YES, but looking back now, the answer was a definite NO. In the booming market of 2007, I was more of an order-taker than a realtor. I sat in open houses seven days a week, and the buyers basically closed themselves because if they didn't buy the house, they knew the next person would. I had zero sales skills but didn't know it.

By the end of 2008, I was coming to my senses. I wasn't selling houses, but I noticed that many of the veteran realtors were. I was putting in more hours, doing more open houses, and driving more clients around, but they were selling houses, and I wasn't. What was going on? The bottom line is that they had sales skills, and I did not. The entry level course I took to get my license didn't teach me any sales skills at all! This realization was my first step to acquiring the skills I needed to be successful.

If I were to ask you what sales skills you have, what would your answer be? Most realtors would say that they are "good with people." That may be true, but it doesn't mean you can sell a house. Ask yourself these questions: Can you do deals in a recession when everyone is running for cover? Can you negotiate? Would your clients refer you to their friends and family? Is everyone happy at the end of a transaction? Answering these questions will help you see where you have room to grow, and my goal in this chapter is to teach you some skills that will help take your business to the next level.

Essential Sales Skills:
Building Trust

People want to work with those they know, like, and trust, and nowhere is this truer than when people are buying or selling their most valuable asset: their homes. If a foundation of trust is there, everything is easier. If you excel at building trust, you will make a lot more money in a lot less time with fewer problems. It will be easier to pick up new clients, keep your old ones, and get referrals. The amount of trust today's consumers put in their realtor is astounding. A survey asked consumers why they chose to work with a certain realtor, and the number one reason was trust, even before experience and the ability to negotiate. It makes so much sense for realtors to invest time and effort into learning how to build trust.

Let's take a step back and think about why most people DON'T trust salespeople. The image most consumers have of a salesperson is a lazy swindler only in it for the commission. It's the few bad apples who are not transparent, who advertise falsely, who fail to communicate and lack empathy that give the honest and diligent people in the sales industry a bad reputation. You know the kind of realtor I'm talking about—the one who advertises a property that is two rows back from the water as "waterfront." I suspect that if you have chosen to read this book, you are not that kind of realtor.

Let's look at the skills needed to build trust during a transaction. Trust is built from two places: the head and the heart. Cognitive trust is from the head, and it comes from our accomplishments, our skills, and our reliability. In other words, are we good at what we do? The second-place trust comes from is the heart, and this is called affective trust. Affective trust is built through empathy and rapport. In other words, do we care about the client and can they tell that we care? Putting it in layman's terms, do you have good chemistry with your clients? Is there a positive vibe you can all feel in the relationship? In order to gain trust, we need to be good at what we do, and we need to care about the people we do it for. Please commit that to memory!

So how do you go about establishing this kind of trust with your clients? Telling people how great you are does not build trust. Instead of TELLING someone how awesome you are, you need to humbly SHOW them by following these seven tips to help you build trust in the field.

1. **Selling is not Telling**

   Too often, salespeople think they need to share all of their knowledge with buyers every chance they get, so they end up doing most of the talking. Influence isn't built this way; it is built through asking questions. People love talking about themselves and the more questions you ask them, the better they feel. When people feel good around you, they will trust your advice and will listen to you.

   We need to remember that today's buyers have more access to information than they ever have before, and I believe this is a good thing. Years ago, realtors used to hold back information, making it necessary for the buyer to look to them as the only one with the knowledge they need. While this may have been effective in the past, it is not so today. In this information generation, buyers have all they need to know at their fingertips. What today's buyers want and need is a guide or consultant to help them through the process of buying or selling a home. Today's realtors need to be question-askers not information-tellers. When we ask questions, we show that we care about the needs of our clients. As the clients answer our questions, they will reveal what actually matters to them and this knowledge will help us serve them better.

Let's use an open house as a hypothetical scenario to show how asking questions can help you build trust.

Scenario 1: Potential buyers walk in; you introduce yourself and proceed to tell them that the house you are in is a wonderful house with three bedrooms, two bathrooms and a nice kitchen. You are all standing in the kitchen when you say this, but you tell them it is nice anyway.

Scenario 2: Potential buyers walk in; you introduce yourself and the conversation goes something like this:

You: "Where are you guys from?"

Them: "Oh, we are from out of town and are looking to maybe move into this area."

You: "That's great! How well do you know this area?"

Them: "Well, the internet says it has a great walk score."

You: "Do you have kids?"

Them: "Yes we do!"

You: "Me too! So how much do good schools matter to you?"

Them: "That's the most important thing for us."

You: "That would be the most important thing for me too. Are you hoping your kids will be walking to school? Because even though the internet says this neighbourhood has a great walk score, there is actually a pretty high crime rate between here and the school."

I'll stop there because I think you can see where I'm going with this. Let's recap. In the first scenario, do you know anything about the clients? Do they feel that they can trust you or that you care about them? Not at all. So far, you are a sales guy treating them like children by telling them that the kitchen you are all standing in is nice. Now let's look at the second scenario. In about the same amount of time, you have demonstrated that you care about their needs and that you know the area better than the internet does. Scenario 2 is much more likely to begin laying a foundation of trust with these potential clients.

2. Be Reliable

Do what you say you are going to do, even in the small things. If you say you are going to send a contract to a client at a certain time, you had better do it. If you say you will follow up with a client tomorrow at 6:00 p.m. you need to follow up tomorrow at 6:00 p.m. This might sound obvious, but reliability is the foundation of trust, so always honour your promises and do everything you say you are going to do. Be the realtor who under-promises and over-delivers, not the one who over-promises and under-delivers. Always be five minutes early and if for some unforeseen reason you are going to be late, always call well in advance. This shows your clients that you are reliable and a real professional.

Being consistent is another way to prove your reliability to clients. Your energy and personality need to be consistent no matter what is going on or how you feel. If you are up and down like a yo-yo, it will be hard for your clients to trust you. Keep your cool and do not get rattled or get upset, even if things get difficult in either the buying or selling process. And never get upset with other realtors who are involved in the transaction. Real estate deals are emotional, and we need to be a rock for our clients throughout the process. So

93

be consistent, and also be yourself. Clients will see through you in a heartbeat if you are pretending to be someone you are not. Be yourself, be professional, be hardworking, and be kind. This will go a long way in building trust.

3. **Communicate Effectively**

In every conversation with your clients, use simple words, not real estate jargon, abbreviations, or acronyms that they might not understand. You might think it makes you look smart, but the best teachers are always the ones who take hard topics and make them simple enough for anyone to understand. Don't call a client's home a unit or listing; it is their home that they are proud of. Every communication is a chance to build that heart connection with your clients, so always make sure your clients understand what you are saying. Ask questions like, "Does that make sense?" or "How does that make you feel?" to make sure they are an active participant in every conversation. Remember, clients should always talk more than you.

4. **Be Honest**

Tell the truth, and when in doubt, disclose! Don't be afraid to tell people that the house they are looking at probably isn't the best fit for their family. This builds trust because it shows your clients that you truly want them to get the best house possible. If something comes out that ends up being your fault, own up to it and never throw other people under the bus or shift the blame. Do not leave out any details about a listing even if you think they don't matter. I knew a realtor who had a listing and knew that someone had died in the house. The rules in our city do not require a disclosure for something like this, so the realtor thought there was no reason to disclose it. Guess what happened? Right after the clients moved in, a neighbor came over and told them that someone had died in the house they had just bought. The clients were very unhappy and no longer trusted that realtor, and the agent lost them as clients.

Always be honest by disclosing the climate of an area in all four seasons. In my city we have a beautiful neighborhood near a huge river. Ninety percent of the year, you can go outside and enjoy the beauty of nature, but for the other 10 percent, right at the beginning of summer, millions and millions of relentless, blood-sucking mosquitos come out. Even if you want to mow your lawn or have a beer on your deck, you have to cover every surface of your body in netting. How do you think your clients would react if they bought the house in winter and you said nothing about the early summer reality of this area? It is always better to disclose everything you know.

Early in my career, I thought I was supposed to know all the answers. When a client would ask me a question, I didn't know the answer to, I would either deflect or make something up. Looking back, I can't believe I did this, and in talking to other realtors, many of them have done the same. We think it is more important to look like we know what we are doing all the time than it is to be honest. Now, when a client asks me a question, I don't know the answer to, I say "I am not sure. Let me make a note of that and get back to you." Then I keep my promise, find out the answer, and promptly get back to them. Honesty builds trust.

5. **Demonstrate your Integrity**

Everyone says they work with integrity, but your clients want you to prove it through your actions. One way to prove your integrity is to keep secrets. If someone tells you something in confidence, keep it confidential. Here is an example: you are with potential clients who are considering listing their home with you. You are at their house giving your listing presentation and you say, "Your neighbors John and Karen sure love this area. I helped them get into their house, even though they didn't think they could afford it. I found them a great mortgage broker who got them a massive loan so they could buy in this neighborhood." You may think you are proving what a great agent you are, but in reality, you are showing that you lack integrity. These potential clients will assume that you will share their personal information with others like you did with John and Karen's, and you will lose their trust and likely the listing.

6. **Be Knowledgeable**

As realtors, not only do we need to know about the product we are selling, we also need to be hyper-aware and conversant about market conditions. Consumers have more information at their fingertips than ever before, but they are still looking for someone to explain to them how everything works. You must be knowledgeable about buyer's vs seller's markets, inventory in the area, days on market, and much more. You need to be a professional at contracts as well. Here is a tip that I have done with excellent results. Early in my career, a wise, older real estate agent told me to memorize every contract I work with so that I can read it upside down while I am sitting across a table from clients. I did, and my clients are consistently blow away by my ability to do this. I can display my skills and knowledge without having to say anything at all. Many of my clients have recommended to their friends that they use their realtor who can read upside down and has every contract memorized!

7. **Ask Questions**

We touched on this already, but I can't stress enough how important this is for building trust. We may think that the more we talk, the more we will show how great we are and the more the client will trust us, but actually doing all the talking has the opposite effect. Ask as many questions as possible and then actually listen to the answers. This displays empathy, and immediately potential clients will begin to trust you. We have two ears and one mouth, which is a great reminder to listen twice as much as we speak!

Always ask relevant and open-ended questions. Here's an example of the same question asked two ways: If you want to know what your client thinks of the house you just toured, and you want to build some trust at the same time, is it better to say, "Does that layout work for you?" or "What did you think about the layout of that house?" The first question will get a yes or no response, and the client will feel like you are being pushy. In the second example, the clients are free to say what they liked and did not like, and you will find out some valuable information in the process. The information will help you serve them better, and at the same time you have shown them that you care what they think, that you really listen to them, and that you want to get them the best possible house. This may seem small, but asking lots of questions, and asking them in the right way will go a long way in building trust. From that foundation of trust will come happy clients, referrals and repeat business.

The Art of Closing

The ability to close is the difference between the top 10 percent of realtors and the other 90 percent. The art of closing has come a long way over the years. Years ago, salespeople had a million different names for closing: "the sharp angle," "the assumption close," and "the alternative option close" to name a few. This old-school way of closing forgot that we are dealing with real, live human beings, and the techniques that worked back then would send buyers running today. When I started my career, no one taught me how to close or what the process was, so I want to pass on to you what I have learned over the years. I want you to be able to close in today's market with today's buyers and sellers.

In order to begin improving your sales skills, you need to put yourself in the buyer's shoes. Learning what it feels like for buyer's when someone is pushy and obviously trying to "close them" is invaluable for every salesperson. The way I learned this was somewhat unconventional, but I highly recommend it! I visited some local car lots posing as a potential buyer and observed how the salespeople worked and how I felt in response to their sales methods. For me, this process helped me learn what not to do, and was the beginning of me learning how to effectively close in real estate.

When I step onto a car lot, I want a certain type of experience. I want some zero-pressure time to walk around the lot to investigate the different vehicles and compare the sticker prices before I ever talk to a salesperson. When I am ready, I want to go into the showroom and talk to someone about going for a test drive in a car that I feel might be what I am looking for. At this point, I am hoping the salesperson doesn't ask me a lot of questions about financing or timing, I just want to experience the car. During the test drive, I want to see if I can trust the salesperson, and I'd also like to hear about some of the features of the vehicle that I may not know about. After the test drive, I'd like the salesperson to recommend that I take a few test drives of the competitors' vehicles, showing me that they have my best interest at heart and want me to make the best decision possible. Then, when I am ready to purchase, I want to feel like I am getting a good deal. I am guessing I have just described your ideal experience of buying a car as well, right? Unfortunately, this is not how it usually plays out.

The more likely scenario is this: you park in the back of the lot somewhere hoping a salesperson doesn't see you. You duck around the vehicles so that you aren't noticed by their constant scanning of the lot. Inevitably, you are spotted anyway, and a salesperson runs out with a big smile, shakes your hand and says

"Wow, this car is really nice" and proceeds to talk about how you should buy something now before you miss out on the great deals. While you are politely trying to find a way to leave, they are asking for your phone number so they can follow up.

I know that car sales and home sales are different, but by visiting car lots, you can boost your sales skills by putting yourself in the buyer's shoes and remembering how it feels when a pushy salesperson tried to "close you." This will help you become a better real estate agent and a better closer.

I have already covered in detail how you can build trust with clients. If someone does not like or trust you, you will have a very hard time closing them, even if you are the most intelligent and knowledgeable person in the room. Never think you can work on the skill of closing without first building a foundation of trust. If you have spent most of your time getting to know your clients and building trust, closing is simply the natural end to the conversation. If you try to close a client without this foundation, I promise it will not be successful and no one will be having a good time.

Let's start by defining exactly what "closing" means and then get into how to do it the right way. Closing is setting up the natural end to the transaction. I prefer to say that closing sets up the natural end to the conversation. Never forget this: all clients want to buy, but they don't want to "be sold." This is such a great saying for many reasons. As a realtor, you need to have the confidence to know that a client actually wants to buy a house and that they are looking for a trusted advisor to help them do so. They don't need or want to be pressured into a sale. A client who feels like you "sold them" will not refer you to their friends and family and are not likely to call you again when they need a realtor in the future. It is not your job to sell them on anything.

The best analogy for closing can be explained through my love of hiking mountains. Ironically, hiking and closing in sales is a very similar experience. The goal of every hike is to get to the summit, just like "closing" is the end of every sales transaction. The only problem is you can't start at the summit, just like you can't start trying to close a human right away. To get to the top of the mountain, you must first start at the bottom. As you gain elevation you will encounter new challenges, and if you have taken the proper route, you will eventually make it to the summit. However, if you take the wrong route your chances of making the summit before dark become very slim. Trust me I have taken some crazy routes hiking mountains, and I kept pushing thinking I could still make the summit. The harder I pushed the worse it got, and often it left me exposed on the side of a sketchy cliff with no options but to go back down. The same goes for closing, except it won't be as dangerous! We must take the correct journey in sales in order to get our prospect to the summit. It is important to know that steps cannot be skipped along the way. Closing looks like this: Step 1 Build Trust; Step 2 Demonstrate Value; Step 3 Qualify the Prospect; Step 4 Present the Product; and Step 5 Close. These are the five basic steps. The time spent on each of these steps is also disproportionate. Most of the time needs to be spent on Step 1. If you picture a mountain, it has a huge base and a small top. Most of your time hiking is spent on the base of the mountain and not on the summit. The summit is the fun part, but it is generally the shortest part of the hike. The same goes with closing. Most of the time needs to be spend on building trust before we move onto anything else. If you try to close quickly it will never work. Everyone has the skill to be a great closer if you take the correct steps. Each of the steps are straightforward.

Step 1: Building Trust. Every salesperson must remember that people want to work with humans they know, like, and trust. Our goal then is to be a likable trustworthy person. We must be easy-going, optimistic, and very curious. The more questions we ask, the more people will like and trust us. A great question to ask to involve people's family, careers, vacations, and future goals. Most people think a salesperson must have the gift of the gab; I would argue a good salesperson must be a skilled question-asker. Remember not to rush this step. Relationship building is our number one objective, and it takes time. People will know if you have ulterior motives, so make sure you drop any expectations. Get to know people because you want too not because you have too.

Step 2: Demonstrate Value. Demonstrating value is done at a buyer's presentation or listing presentation. This must be in person! We must be able to show how we add value to any transaction. We will dive deeper into this in the following pages.

Step 3: Qualify the Prospect. Every buyer and seller should be qualified before you move to the next step. I always recommend getting your prospect to use one of your financing contacts to confirm they are qualified for what they say they are. I have learned this the hard way too many times early in my career. I would trust that a buyer was qualified to $300,000, then I would show them houses, and write an offer only to have it all fall apart last minute because they weren't qualified for what they said they were.

Step 4: Presenting the Product. This is just Showing Properties to your qualified prospects. I call this part "shopping with friends." This is one of my favourite parts. It is fun seeing different properties and experiencing how people live in their homes. I have experienced so many memorable moments from showing houses, but one stands out. We once went into a house where the seller was outside on the porch smoking a pipe and siting on an old rocking chair. As we entered the home, they warned us that their spouse had passed away and their soul had travelled into their pet parrot. I couldn't tell if they were joking or not, so we slowly entered the house. As we walked through the home, the parrot followed us and kept screeching with the words, "I am watching you, I am watching you!" The hair on our necks stood up and we couldn't get out of the house fast enough. It was so freaky and definably turned the buyers off. We did however get a good laugh in the vehicle on the way to the next showing. Obviously, there are important nuances and skills to showing homes that we will go over in the following pages.

Step 5: Close. If you have skillfully done all these steps properly the close will be the easiest part. Most buyers or sellers will close themselves if you have coached them properly. They will know the parameters of the transaction and where the natural end of the road should be.

Now that we know that "closing" is simply the natural end to the conversation, let's get practical and learn how to improve your closing skills.

The Principles of Closing

1. **Help the buyer set reasonable expectations.**
   The first step to setting up the natural end to a conversation is to take control of the situation. If your clients are buyers, you must do a buyer's presentation and if they are sellers, you must sit down at the kitchen table for a listing presentation. We will look at these presentations in detail later in the chapter, but for now what is important to note is that these presentations are where the "close" begins. When all parties know the expectations of the transaction, closing becomes a team approach: a win-win situation.

   Here is how closing (setting up the natural end to the conversation) works for buyers. At the buyer's presentation, I set up the close right at the beginning by talking to my clients about the three main factors involved in buying their dream home: price, location, and floor plan. I ask them what is most important to them in the initial meeting. Often buyers will say they want the best location, but after a tour they find that they prefer to move farther away to get a nicer, cheaper house. At this point they likely don't really know, but this process is so valuable for me to build rapport, and if there are two parties involved in the sale, to gauge their relationship and discover what is important to each of them. One will say they want a big kitchen, while the other says they want to live in the best location. This gives me the opportunity to explain that they will only ever get two of the three (price, location, floor plan). For example, if you want a great location, the price will be higher, and the plan will typically be smaller. If you want a bigger floor plan, the price will be higher, or you will have to move farther from the good location. Listening to them talk about what is important to them shows that I care, and that I am on their team, working hard to find them the right home.

After explaining the two out of three principles, I talk about the "80 % Rule." This is another way to help buyers set reasonable expectations. No one will ever find the perfect house, and we need to help our clients realize that if we find a house that suits 80 percent of their needs, it is "perfect." Evidence for this rule can be found in people who build custom homes. When I tour my clients' dream homes, every one of them tells me about all the things they wished they had done differently. I can attest to this personally! I have regrets about every custom home I have ever built. Our job as realtors is to keep our clients realistic. If you feed into their belief that you will find them the "perfect" house, you will be showing houses every day of your life and have a ton of disappointed buyers. Perfection is the last thing you should be chasing. An 80 percent house is exactly what your clients are looking for. Remember, timing is everything! This conversation must be at the buyer's presentation. If you tell the buyers after twenty-five showings that they should only be looking for an 80 percent house, they will feel like you are giving up and don't believe you can find them the best house. Being clear from the start helps your client set reasonable expectations and sets the stage for a team approach where everyone wins. This system helps eliminate any sense of "me vs the buyer" or of me trying to "close them." It has us working as a team to find them the right home. More often than not, the buyers will call me after a buyer's tour and say they found their 80 percent house, and they would like to put in an offer. By helping them set realistic expectations, the buyers just sold themselves. It really can be that easy.

2. **Anticipate and handle future objections.**

Have you heard of the ghost of real estate? I sure hadn't. Picture this: you are in an open house, a beautiful home in the perfect area. The house is clean, well decorated, and in the right school district. The market is falling, but you think people would be crazy not to buy this house. *This is money in the bank,* you think to yourself. *I will sell this house this weekend.* As the buyers come through, they keep saying the same thing. "Wow, this house is beautiful, but we need to think about it." And you say, "Great! Think about it, and let me know" because you don't want to appear pushy. But what happens next? They never contact you again, and if you reach out, they give you some excuse for not wanting to buy the house. My friends, you have just seen the ghost in real estate: you may not be able to see it, but you know it is there.

During the housing crash of 2008 I had done what many immature realtors do. I spent all my money on a fancy car and badly needed a sale to pay for my new lifestyle. I was so desperate in fact, that I had what I call "commission breath," which I am sure potential clients could smell a mile away! No one wants to work with a desperate salesperson. I was doing open houses seven days a week and all the buyers kept saying the same thing: "It's a beautiful home, but we will have to think about it." I was scared of being that pushy salesperson, so I would say "Absolutely! I would want to sleep on it too." But the clients weren't calling back and if I followed up with them, they would tell me the house was not for them. I had officially met my first "ghost": I knew there was a problem, but I couldn't see it or touch it, so I couldn't do anything about it.

The reality was that I had no skills to handle client objections. During any recession or dip in real estate, the objections increase, which is why so many agents struggle in these markets. If agents had a full understanding of how to handle objections, they would find it much easier to make consistent sales even when the market is slow.

Before getting any deeper into the skill of anticipating and handling objections, it is important to note that a good real estate agent must always be willing to advise their clients to walk away from a deal if their objection is too big. We never want to let our clients make a bad decision.

The first way to objection-handle is to avoid the objection altogether by anticipating it before it appears. If you can prepare your client in advance for potential issues that may arise, then objections will no longer kill deals. Here is an example: you are showing homes that were built in the early 1990s. We all know that in the early 90s many homes were built with Poly-B piping, which is notorious for causing plumbing leaks, and most insurance companies will either refuse to give you insurance or the premiums will be really high. This is a fairly major issue. Here are two potential scenarios:

Scenario 1:

When showing your client homes built in the early 90s, you do not educate them about Poly-B plumbing, and the home inspection is the only thing between you and a closed deal. How do you think your client will respond when this plumbing issue shows up on the inspection? They will very likely back out of the deal after calling their Uncle Bob who tells them Poly-B is a huge issue and that their realtor should never have got them into this deal in the first place. You have now lost your clients' trust and you have a huge uphill battle to try not to lose both the deal and good clients. No matter how good your objection handling skills are, at this point the clients and family members will trust you a little less, making your job that much harder. There is a better alternative.

Scenario 2:

Same client (let's call her Suzie), same house, same Poly-B issue. But this time, you have educated her in advance. It's a simple two-minute conversation and it goes like this:

"Suzie, I'm going to show you some houses that were built in the early 90s. These houses are great because of the location, price, and the big backyards that you love. However, I need to warn you that many of them contain Poly-B piping, which is a product that was eventually recalled because it caused plumbing leaks in many homes. If the temperature gets above 130 degrees or the joints were done incorrectly, the chances of leaks are even higher. We will find out in advance what plumbing is in the home and make sure the seller is willing to fix this or have a plumber give you a quote, which we will ask the seller to take off the purchase price. Usually, it runs around $10,000 to fix this issue. How do you feel about all of this, Suzie?" Most likely, Suzie will thank you for letting her know and will be happy you are so knowledgeable and will say that she feels good about looking at these homes anyway.

Now, when you find a house that Suzie loves that happens to have Poly-B piping, it will not turn into a deal-killing objection because you have prepared her in advance. Even more importantly, you will have earned her trust, and the chance of a referral is high. Another lesson we can learn from these scenarios is how beneficial it is to be extremely knowledgeable about common issues in the area you are selling in.

The most common objection we hear from clients is "I want to think about it" because it is the easiest way to avoid sales pressure. People get overwhelmed easily during the buying process, and it can be difficult to find the root of their stall, in other words, to isolate their objection. One way to do this is to remember the three main objections to buying a house are price, floor plan, and location. Let's do an oversimplified conversation that will help you isolate and handle the "I want to think about it" objection. Remember that an actual conversation like this will involve more open-ended questions and lots of empathetic listening.

You: Do you want to buy this house?

Buyer: I am not sure. I want to think about it.

You: That makes sense. I would to! Do you like the location?

Buyer: Yes, I love the location!

You: Do you like the floor plan?

Buyer: I love the floor plan! It works perfectly for our family.

You: Awesome. Well, if it was $100,000 less would you buy it?

Buyer: Yes, we would write an offer today.

You have successfully isolated the buyer's objection: price. And you still have a chance to sell the home. It is really important not to leave it at "I have to think about it" because you will likely lose them to another realtor who is more skilled at handling objections.

Another objection to anticipate is cold feet/buyer's remorse. For first-time buyers, I call it cold feet, and for everyone else I call it buyer's remorse. It is the negative feeling we get in our bodies after making a large decision, like purchasing a home. This can be very difficult to deal with in real estate as you are working against the anatomy of the human brain. There is nothing worse than working hard to get a good deal for your clients only to have them come to you in a week and say they want to back out of the deal. They will typically give an excuse like they are afraid of what the market is going to do or that their mom thinks it is a bad idea. If this happens to you, I want to tell you that it's your fault. You heard me right. If you failed to prepare your client in advance for the buyer's remorse they will experience after they make the largest purchase of their lives, it is your fault. We need to objection-handle in the buyer's meeting right at the beginning, long before it becomes an objection.

This is how I prepare my clients for cold feet at all of my buyer's presentations. I tell them this story because there is such power in a story:

I will never forget my wedding day. My bride was amazing and wonderful and the girl I wanted to spend the rest of my life with, but when she was walking down the aisle, I was panicking. I started sweating and swaying from side to side, and I am pretty sure no blood was getting to my hands or feet because I couldn't feel them. I knew I was making the right choice, but my body was freaking out. Thoughts raced through my head, and I wanted to run. Simply put, I got cold feet.

I end the story by asking them to please call me when they feel this because they will! Our clients are typically making the largest investment of their entire lives. You have no idea how many phone calls I get the day before the contract is finalized from my clients telling me how right I was about them getting cold feet They always tell me they are so glad I told them to expect it because they were prepared for it and are now excited to move forward. This is a much better conversation to have than your clients calling to say they are backing out of the deal because their friend/cousin/grandma said it was a bad idea.

The ability to anticipate and handle your client's objections is a vital sales skill that is worth spending time developing.

3. **Never lose a close deal again.**

How many deals have you had fall apart at the last minute? The buyer hit their limit and wouldn't come up any more or your seller gets frustrated and won't budge an inch. Losing close deals costs us so much time and money because you have to go to work to find that buyer another property or find that seller another offer. If you miss three close deals a year and the average commission is $10,000, then you have missed out on $30,000, or you've had to work many more hours for the same amount of money. Learning how to put close deals together is a skill that will elevate your business.

As a young agent, I really struggled with putting close deals together, and I could never put my finger on why. I would have buyers that would jump up and down over a property, claiming it was the house of their dreams, only to stop $5,000 dollars short in negotiation and tell me they wanted to walk away from the deal. Just twenty-four hours ago, it was the house of their dreams and now they were mad at the seller and wanted to walk away.

Exasperated after one of these experiences, I walked into the office of one of my mentors (let's call her Katie) and complained about these crazy clients I had. Katie smiled and calmly asked me a question: "How many people are involved in this transaction?" I looked at her and said, "Two. The buyer and the seller." Katie smiled and said, "Actually, there are four parties: the buyer and the buyer's agent, and the seller and the seller's agent. Why don't you get all the parties to work together?" I had never thought about it like this before. The buyer wants to buy, and the seller wants to sell so why not work together so that everyone gets what they want? She told me that I needed to be a little less emotional and look for a win-win. She pointed out that the other realtor was not my adversary, but rather a dealmaker just like me. We are on the same team, trying to find a way for all parties to win.

I asked Katie how I could break the standstill in the deal that was threatening to fall apart. The buyer would not go up and the seller refused to come down.

"Here's an idea," she said. "Ask your buyer to come up $2,000 dollars instead of the $5,000 the seller wants. And say that you will give up $500 dollars of your commission to bring it to $2,500. Then call the other realtor and ask them to do the same."

I had nothing to lose so I tried it, and guess what happened? It worked! It was so easy, it almost felt wrong. All parties involved gave a little, and everyone got the outcome they wanted. I had happy customers and the deal got done. To this day, I teach all my students this valuable lesson. There are four parties to every sales transaction and all parties want to make a deal happen. We just need to find a way to get there. Close deals just need a leader, and that should be you. Some realtors might take offence at giving away some of their hard-earned commission, and in theory, I don't disagree. You should never offer to give away part of your commission if you don't have to. But when a deal is close and negotiations have stagnated, this is one way to get the deal done.

This might sound like a simple concept, but in the moment, it was a profound learning experience for me. I thought my job was to fight with every realtor to get the best deal for my clients. What I didn't realize was that my emotions were negatively affecting the whole transaction. My client treated the transaction like a win/lose because that's the message I was sending. I would say things like "Wow, that seller is difficult. They aren't budging an inch," or "I don't trust that realtor." This negativity was affecting my ability to close deals and have happy clients. My mentor, a veteran realtor, could see the problem a mile away.

Katie's advice showed me that I needed to take a new approach. No more "us against them" messaging. Speak highly of all parties involved. When you write an offer or receive an offer, tell your clients that the other realtor seems really great and that you are excited to work with them. This will make the whole negotiation process a positive one. After all, the transaction is a win/win situation: buyers want to buy a home that they can enjoy, and sellers want to sell so they can move on to their next opportunity. So, stay positive!

This type of situation comes up in slower markets or falling markets or with a unique property. In a busy, rising market, you won't have the same issues putting close deals together because the fear of missing out drives buyers to pay what the seller wants. But if you have a unique property or you are in a soft market, you need to be ready to lead all four parties into bringing the deal together. In some cases, I have given up to half of my commission away to save a deal.

This situation also happens far more frequently with sellers. The seller loves their home, but underestimates how fast the market is dropping, or the seller needs a certain amount out of their home to be able to clear title. As realtors, we know that in a soft market, if they don't get a deal done today, a month from now, they won't be able to sell at all. When the seller receives an offer, I don't want to mess around and risk losing the deal, so I am willing to give up something so all parties can win. When you learn the skill of getting all parties to work together, you will have happy customers and save yourself a lot of time.

Now I want to share some more practical closing techniques that I have found to be very effective, and I know you will too.

4. **The "Reduce to the Ridiculous" close.**
This was actually the first type of close I ever learned. I learned this originally from a great teacher named Tom Hopkins, and I have modified it for today's buyers. At the beginning of your conversation (during the buyer's presentation or the listing presentation, which I deal with in detail later in the chapter) you need to warn your buyers about a sales technique you are going to use on them. This is what I say, always with humour to keep the conversation really light-hearted:

Me: "Mrs. and Mr. Buyer, if we are close to a deal but we are still apart by $10,000 to $50,000 (or whatever amount fits that particular potential deal), then be prepared because I am going to use my cheesy closing line on you!"

The Buyers: They laugh and say "Okay, what is it?"

Me: "Say we are $10,000 apart, and I think it's a great house for you. I will reduce that number to the ridiculous. Let's say interest rates are 4% and for every $100,000 you borrow the cost is $526 per month. This would mean that $10,000 mortgaged over twenty-five years is only $52.60 per month. If I reduce this further, that is $1.75 dollars per day, which adds up to about 2 Starbucks drinks per week. I'm going to say to you, 'Mr. and Mrs. Buyer, would you be willing to give up 2 Starbucks per week to buy this amazing house'?"

The Buyers: "Of course we would be willing to do that!"

It's crazy simple, but this works with both buyer and sellers! As long as you set this up in advance, you should never lose a close deal again. However, I have a few warnings for you if you use this close. The first is, DO YOUR MATH RIGHT! If your math is wrong, you will look like an idiot and your clients will never trust you again. Secondly, do not use this close in the moment if you have not warned them ahead of time that you will use it. It will come off as pushy and cheesy and you will lose trust immediately.

5. **The "Crappy Listing in the Future" closing line.**

This is my favourite line, and I want to you steal it. Not that I believe in scripts or memorization, but this closing line immediately improved my ability to sell. Here it is:

"Mr. and Mrs. Buyer, I need you to know that selfishly, I want to find you a great house, so I am not stuck with a crappy listing in the future."

More often than not, this makes them laugh, and they say it makes them feel better. There are two things I love about this line: one is the raw honesty of it, and the other is the intention for the future. The raw honesty lets the buyer know that their realtor has selfish intentions, but that those intentions are going to work in their favour and get them a great house. This line really works, but I do not want you to take advantage of it or use it lightly. Your job is to be incredibly trustworthy and build clients for life. Only use this line if you truly want to find the best home for your clients. The bonus for you is a great house to sell when they call you to list again in the future. Another win-win.

The Listing and Buyer's Presentations

Did you know that 60 percent of realtors don't have a listing presentation or a buyers' presentation and 30 percent of realtors only use them some of the time? The last 10 percent of realtors use one every single time, which explains why the top 20 percent of agents sell 80 percent of the homes.

Listing Presentations 101

If you want to consistently be a top agent, a good listing presentation is non-negotiable. It can be a game-changer for any agent and can help even a new agent get a listing over a twenty-year veteran.

There is an art to meeting people in their homes with the purpose of convincing them to let you represent them as their agent. Anyone can learn these skills, so let's look at how you can make your own great listing presentation or make your existing one better.

1. Booking the Appointment

Getting an appointment is a skill in itself. When someone indicates that they might be interested in selling, your number one goal is to get a meeting in person, at the seller's house. Often, you will have a small objection right off the bat like they don't think they are ready to sell, or they don't want to waste your time so can you just tell them what their house is worth or what your commission rate is. You need to effectively avoid answering these questions (while making sure they know you are not ignoring their feelings) and get that meeting booked. We have already established that step one in any sales process is building trust, and meeting at the seller's home is vital to this step. If you can get an in-person meeting, your chances of getting the listing are much higher.

Here are some helpful ways to overcome objections to an in-person, in-home meeting. If a potential client tells you they are thinking of selling, say, "I would love to stop by for a quick forty-five minutes to give you the best information as you and your family make this important decision." (This addresses their potential objection that they may not be ready to list). Tell them that you will go over how you market a property, what the current market is doing, and what their home is worth in today's market conditions. Assure them that it will be a zero-pressure meeting because your client's matter, and you will always do what is best for them. Give them a choice of a couple days and times, giving yourself enough time to prepare for the meeting, while making sure it is within the next two days. If you book them a week out, they will have the chance to get cold feet or talk to friends and family who will recommend five other realtors. Avoid saying the too open-ended "when does it work for you?" because this invites the answer "I will let you know." You also need to be careful with your words. Do not commit to anything like price, commission, or say what you think they want to hear. Communicate that you must go through their home to give them the best, most accurate advice. At this point they will say things like, my house is a mess, or we aren't ready. You say, "no problem" (which is my favourite words to show I understand their feelings) and then I say that I have seen a million messy houses, and I can look past it, so would Monday at 4:00pm work? This works almost every time. If at this point, they say only next week works, make sure you say "no problem, I will see you then" or you will come across as pushy.

Once you get an in-person meeting at their home, give yourself a pat on the back because you are ahead of most of the competition! You have set a meeting where the seller feels no pressure and has an understanding of what to expect from you.

2. **Prepare for your Meeting**

You must have three things ready to go before the meeting: 1) The comparable stats of the property 2) The stats of the local market and 3) The presentation of value when they choose to work with you.

First, the comparables used to find the value of the seller's home. If you are a new agent, I always recommend asking a more experienced agent to help you with these. There are some basic rules to follow. Comparables should not go more than three months back as the market is always changing, and always make sure to compare apples to apples. For example, do not compare a three-story home to a two-story home, or an apartment in the downtown area to one twenty miles away. When we compare, we want to get age, square footage, bedrooms, bathrooms, and type of house calculated correctly. Also, it is important to find all of the sales in their area in the last year, so you are not surprised when the seller says their neighbour sold for ten million dollars last year. Sellers know a lot about their neighborhood, and they will lose trust if they know something that you don't. I also need to stress the importance of knowing the value of a property. Remember it is "sold" prices that dictate value not the "active listing" prices. If their neighbour lists his house for $1 million, it doesn't mean he will get it. I always let my clients know that I am not here to list a property, I am here to sell a property. If they only want it listed, they are free to call anyone they want, but when they want to sell, then I will be their person.

The next thing I bring is the current market stats. This includes the number of houses sold in the area, the number of active listings in the area, the average prices in the area, and the absorption rate of homes in the area. I use these stats to educate my seller on the type of market we are working in (seller's, buyer's or balanced). Having these current market stats goes a long way in building trust with your clients and is a great way to demonstrate your market knowledge.

Lastly, is your presentation of value, which must be prepared well in advance as it will be used in every listing presentation. In your presentation of value, you will include things like how you market the property, where you spend your money, what makes you unique as a realtor, and your basic biography. It is always awkward talking about yourself, so it is much easier to have a biography and testimonials in the listing presentation for the seller to read after your meeting.

I am a bit old-school, so I provide a listing presentation in a booklet I have put together that summarizes all of the value I will bring to the sale of their home.

3. **Executing the Listing Presentation Meeting**

Congratulations! You have set a time, you have done all of your homework, and you are on your way to meet the clients at their home. Execution of this meeting is so important, and you need to make sure that your vibe is right from the very first moment. We are all drawn to people who are happy, confident, and positive, so it's important to be in this frame of mind. Sellers judge you from the start, so make sure you are dressed professionally but not too formally. For example, I don't recommend a three-piece suit or a designer dress (unless you work in an upscale market). I always wear a blue dress shirt (because studies have shown that blue is a colour that represents trust), jeans, and some good quality shoes when I am meeting a client for the first time.

Smartly dressed and in a happy, confident, and positive frame of mind, you are pulling up to the house. Never use the driveway as this is for friends and family and you have not built that relationship yet. It shows a lot of respect if you park at the curb and walk up their driveway, and it also gives you the opportunity to look at the curb appeal of their home. Make sure to exit your car in an organized fashion, in other words, no fast-food wrappers or papers fall out when you open the door. Sellers are nervous, and I promise you, many of them will be peeking out of a window, watching you pull up. Once you are at the front door, ring the doorbell, and then take a step back and stand sideways, especially if you are a big guy. Once, I had a new agent working for me who is the kindest, gentlest person in the world, but he loves the gym and is as big as a bull! On his first listing, he walked right up to the door, banged on it, and stood with his shoulders squared while the small-statured seller opened the door. He stuck out his hand and shook the seller's hand with a crushing grip, booming out "nice to meet you!"

Before he even got back to the office after that meeting, I got an angry call from the seller saying an intimidating realtor came to their house today and they would not be listing with our company. It's a funny story, and he is now a very successful realtor, but we can learn a lot from it about how to present yourself to clients.

Okay, back to your listing presentation. The seller answers the door, and you kindly introduce yourself and compliment them on some specific part of their house. Make sure you don't come across as cheesy. Make a sincere comment on something you notice and like about their house. One example would be to say, "I like the brickwork on your driveway. It looks awesome." Next, you need to take control of the situation right away without being pushy. You must get to the kitchen table. Something that always works for me is to say, "I have a lot of paperwork, is it ok if we go to the kitchen table so I can spread everything out?" If you don't take control, you will end up on the couch, and it is not an understatement to say that the second you sit down on a couch, you have lost the listing, so never let this happen! The kitchen is so important because it becomes the home base for making business decisions together while giving you room to spread out all of your documents. So, get to the kitchen table, put down your things and then ask for a tour of the house.

Early in my career, I had a listing presentation where everything went wrong. Past clients called me to list a house I had sold them a few years earlier. She was a dancer, and he was a professional kickboxer, and I had met them in an open house and converted them to buyers a few years before. They were memorable clients and a lot of fun to work with, so I was excited for the opportunity to sell their home. When I arrived, I asked to head to the kitchen table, but they were insistent on the living room, so I said okay. Mistake number one. The living room held one love seat and a special massaging chair, the kind that locks around your legs and arms and vibrates everywhere. I thought it would be odd for the three of us to squish onto the love seat, so I sat down in the massage chair. Mistake number two.

Within thirty seconds of me sitting down, the client had a cold beer in my hand. Mistake number three. I was on a runaway train and the afternoon was only getting started. I thanked him for the beer and complimented the cool massage chair. Why I complimented that chair, I have no idea! I should have said something about what a great space their living room was, or how nice the view out their window was, but I chose the massage chair. Mistake number four. It turns out they had never been so proud of anything as they were of that chair. They asked me if any part of my body was sore, and, wanting to keep the conversation going, I said that my lower back had been a bit sore lately. They couldn't have been more excited. The wife jumped to her feet and came over to clamp my legs and one arm into the appropriate spots, leaving one hand free to hold my beer. She pushed the start button, and both of them leaned forward, beaming at me as I enjoyed the pleasures of their new chair. The massage started light, so I took the opportunity to begin talking about the current market conditions. They barely heard me. They were only interested in seeing me enjoy the beer and the massage. Wanting to show my appreciation, I attempted to take a drink as the chair shook violently from side to side. I smiled with a trickle of beer running down my chin and said "Wow, what a nice chair! This is really helping my back." Mistake number five.

Now the dancer and the kickboxer were totally committed to solving my back problem once and for all. Without warning, he turned off the chair, and she unclamped my legs and grabbed my beer. They told me to follow them down to the basement where they had an even more effective tool for back problems. I had no choice but to follow, and at this point had lost count of the number of mistakes I had made in this meeting.

We arrived in a windowless room at the very back of their basement, full of equipment, most of which I had never seen before. Right in the middle of the room sat my fate. They brought me over to this big black machine with straps and long black rods. She told me to stand still while she fastened my legs into the machine. As she was doing this, the kickboxer was reassuring me that it will feel weird at first, but just give in to it and breathe deeply. Now I was nervous, but my legs were already firmly strapped in, so I had no chance of escape. I was wondering how I had ended up down here while my phone and folder full of glossy pages were upstairs, when they said, "here we go!" and flipped me upside-down and locked my body into place. Instantly, the blood rushed to my head, and the pressure behind my eyeballs started to build. The couple were giving me encouragement to relax, to just breathe and asking if I could feel the pressure releasing from my back. I would have agreed to anything at this point if only they would unlock me, so I played it cool and said "Yes, this feels great," even though I felt like my head was going to explode. Ten seconds went by and then thirty and I was starting to get a bit panicked, so I said casually, "I think I am ok now, why don't you flip me back up?"

Then the worst thing that could have possibly happened, happened. The doorbell rang. In a flash, they both went upstairs to answer the door. Now the panic really started to set in. I was sweating profusely, and the pressure behind my eyes was almost unbearable. Things were going blurry, and I started feeling like I was going to pass out.

Upstairs I could hear laughter. A neighbor had popped in for a quick visit. I desperately tried to reach up to my ankles and get the straps off, but they were locked in tight. I considered screaming for help. I wondered if you could die from being left upside-down for too long. (I googled it later, and the answer is yes, by the way). Fifteen minutes ticked by, then twenty. I could no longer see. My only option was to scream for help, never mind what the neighbour would think hearing screams coming from their basement. How had my life turn into this moment? Upstairs, there was a lull in the conversation, which was my cue to start screaming, but before I could, the door flew open and the couple ran in, saying, "Oh my goodness, are you ok?"

I don't remember how we got there, but we ended up at the kitchen table signing the listing. I put my finger near the bottom of every page indicating where they needed to initial, and they complied without question.

Back in my truck, I reclined the seat until my vision came back enough for me to drive. Back at the office, the secretary looked at me and said, "Yikes! Are you okay? You look like you're on drugs!" I went to the bathroom and looked in the mirror to see what she was talking about. My eyes were completely bloodshot, and I had burst all the capillaries under my eyes. It took weeks to get back to looking normal, but I had somehow managed, against all odds, to get that listing.

I hope you now agree with the importance of getting to the kitchen table for your listing presentation!

Funny story aside, the process of how you conduct a listing presentation is very important. As a salesperson you must build relationship, demonstrate value, find out seller motivation and close is a short period of time. This is why this is a skill that needs to be learned and perfected over time.

After we get to the kitchen table, we need to move on to the next step of the presentation. The next step is called the house tour but is used for three necessary things. This includes learning everything about the house, building rapport, and finding out the seller's motivation in a non-invasive way. After we leave our paperwork on the table, and before you sit down, you need to ask for a tour of the house. I always have a notepad with me, but you can have any kind of writing devise that you want. Ask the sellers to show you everything about their house including what they like and don't like. Typically, the decision-maker will show themselves in this moment. They will take the lead on the house tour and lead you through the home that they are so proud of. Take as many notes as possible and ask a lot of questions. The more you write down, the more you will build trust with the sellers. Remember people are fiercely proud of their home and if you take the time to ask questions and take notes it will build huge amounts of trust and rapport. It also shows you care about the details and will properly represent their home. I find sellers will tell you everything in this moment. They tell you about renovations, costs, age of roofs, and HVAC systems without any pressure. In every room make sure you pause and write down things like size of windows, flooring, how the room feels and anything else you can think of. These notes will serve as a guide for your write-up later as well. The goal is to go through the entire property outside and in. I also ask question about the neighbourhood and why they like it. Truthfully the reason they bought the home is probably the reason another family will buy the home. The next goal of the home tour is to find out the seller's motivation. If you look someone in the eye that you just met and ask why they are moving they probably won't tell you, especially because trust hasn't been built yet. However, as a salesperson we need to know this answer to see if the listing is worth taking or not. So this is what I do every time and it works amazingly. You should do the same. If it's a two-storey home, I usually wait for the moment we start walking up the stairs; if it's a one-level, I ask the question the moment I am done the tour and heading back to the kitchen table. Here is the question I ask. I say this is such a beautiful house, why on earth would you want to move? Burn this question into your mind. Almost every time the seller will tell me exactly what their motivation is. You will hear things like we love our house, but we have another kid on the way, or we love our home, but our kids are going to college, and we want to follow them, or we love the house, but we just got offered a better job across the country. You can see the point I am making. The seller will feel disarmed and tell you their exact motivation. If it's a motivation that makes sense, then you take the listing if you get the opportunity. However, if they say well, we like our home, but we just wanted to see what else is out there, then you know their motivation is low. A listing like that is still ok to take, but it better be priced sharp, and you must be willing to work with sellers that will cancel at any time. After you have finished the house tour, head back to the kitchen table for the rest of the listing presentation. You can start the next portion of your presentation knowing the seller's motivation, with a higher level of rapport and better information on the home. These three things are key for the next section of the presentation.

After we sit down, I tell the sellers that I am going to break up the next portion of time into three sections. First, how I sell a house, second, what the current market conditions are, and third, what their home is worth in the current market. Do you notice how I never attach my emotional opinion to value;

I only build a case of the market conditions and how they affect the value of a property. This keeps me and the sellers on the same team instead of a me vs them approach.

How I sell a house. This part is unique because you can do whatever you want. You are an entrepreneur and can be as diverse and creative as you want in selling a home. I care less about what you do and more about how you communicate it. As time goes on and technology changes the way we sell homes will always be changing. What doesn't change is our responsibility to be cutting edge and explain how what we do helps sell homes. Most sellers think realtors put a sign on the property and then walk away until it is sold. They don't realize how much time, effort, and expense goes into every sale. Therefore, it is our job to communicate how we invest (very important word to use) in the sale of their home. You need to know exactly how much you spend on every listing and why you do what you do. Your job then is to break down everything you do and explain why you do it and the cost associated with it. This can be things like video, social media, professional pictures, signs, newspapers, fliers, websites, open houses, and anything else that you want to do. For example, after I go through everything I do and why I do it, I share that my average cost per listing is $2,750 (this is calculated in my review session every year). Knowing how much you "invest" in the sale of a home is powerful information to convey to your potential client. First, it shows that you are a professional who isn't afraid of spending money, and secondly, they will think twice about cancelling a listing because they now know how much time and effort you put into the sale of their home.

The next step of the listing presentation is the market update. This is the time when we demonstrate our expertise of the current market conditions. Often people think they know what the market is doing because of the news or the information they read online, but in reality, they have no clue. Your job is to break down the microclimate of where they live and how it affects the sale or purchase of a home in a particular area or time. Every neighbourhood and price range is unique regardless of the macro conditions. For example, the economy might be crashing in the country, but a small town might have a huge new industry moving in like a Tesla factory or Amazon station, which completely changes the housing market. I will teach in more detail later in the book, but this is the time to teach your potential client about the local market. You will need to tell them if it's a buyer's market, seller's market, or balanced market. You will need to show if the market values are rising or falling, and finally you will want to show the number of unit sales in the last few months and what the average days on market is doing. We are trying to inform our clients about the market so that they can make the best decision for themselves. When a seller is better informed about the market, they will be more reasonable and easier to work with. It will be like working on the same team to make decisions, rather than working against each other. After you have done a good job of teaching the market conditions you now have permission to get into the evaluation side of the presentation.

The market evaluation. This is the moment that the seller has been waiting for. No matter who they are, they want to know what their house is worth, and they will lean into this part of the presentation. Many sellers can be unreasonable with what they think their home is worth, but deep down they usually know, so I want you to be as honest and straightforward in this part of the presentation. Telling the seller what they want to hear to buy a listing will do no one any favours. (P.S. Buying a listing is when you tell a seller the home is worth more than it is so that they like you and list with you.) The strategy for these realtors is to get the listing then start beating the sellers up for price reductions. I personally hate this strategy and think it's a bad and dishonest way to do business. So to start this section you need to first confirm all of the information is correct about their current home. This is where you pull the history of it, a tax search, and any other relevant information. You want to show the seller you have done all of the necessary homework on their property and have not missed any details. Next you will usually use the comparative analysis to get a value for their home. This is comparing apples to apples. It is important to note that sales dictate value not active listings. Just because a neighbour lists their home for $10 million dollars does not mean your house is worth the same. You also must compare similar style homes in similar areas. A two-bedroom home is not a comparable to a four-bedroom home. If you have trouble with this, you should ask a high production realtor in your office to help you.

My goal is usually to find four to six comparable sales and then find five comparable active listings to show where the competition is at. Make sure not to have too many comparables, or you will confuse people, but you also need enough to build a business case of value. There are other ways of appraising value, but for the average realtor this is more than enough. If the market conditions are falling, then you want to price the house below the last sale and below any competition. If the market is rising, then you can list above the last sale but will still need to be below the competition. After you have gone through the comparables, I want to you write down on a piece of paper what you think the market will pay for the house in the current moment. It is important to not say "I think the value is blank" as you don't want to create an emotional connection to the value. You want the value of the property to be connected to the market conditions and not your biased emotional opinion. This will also help the sellers and you be on the same team rather than adversaries when trying to figure out the listing price. After you have written down the estimated value, I want you to do a net sheet.

A net sheet is a simple form that helps the seller know how much they will be left with after they sell their home. This is where you add in all the costs of selling. Often sellers underestimate what is left after a completed sale and realtors are too afraid to do the numbers. This is also the time that you bring up commission. This is important because you have built trust, demonstrated expertise, and have a plan to sell their home. At this point you have built all the value needed to rationalize your commission. This is why you bring up commissions now instead of in the beginning. A net sheet will really cement you as a professional and your clients will appreciate it. Having accurate numbers will help your sellers make the best possible decision with clear parameters. There is nothing worse than a seller who sells their home only to be disappointed they can't afford another house that they thought they could. Remember our goal is to have clients for life and this is done through good advice and expertise.

Mutual decisions. The next step I call mutual decisions. This is where you ask the seller what they think their property is worth. Hopefully the seller trusted your evaluation and coming to an agreement on price is easy. Sometimes (often) the seller will say, "I agree it's worth $600,000, but we want to try $650,000." This is where the decision becomes mutual. You can decide to take the listing for higher, or walk away, or come up with another solution. If I have a seller that wants to do this, then I will take the listing if there is motivation and a discussion that we all know the value is lower. I have this discussion so that I can set up the path for reducing the price in the future. Remember, closing is just creating a natural end to a conversation so this is what we do. It sounds something like this: I am ok with listing your property at $650,000 even though its only worth roughly $600,000 in today's market. Why don't we try for the first fourteen days then reduce to $609,900 so we don't miss the honeymoon stage? The honeymoon stage is when buyers are excited about new inventory and are most likely to buy a property. The seller will usually agree, and now we have made a mutual decision. At the end of the mutual decisions, you are basically at the finish line, but you have one final question to ask. This will be your only hard closing question, but I need you to ask it. Most agents will do a great listing presentation but are too scared to ask for the listing at the end. I don't want you to be that person. I want you to look directly at the decision-maker in the room and say, "Would you like to list with me?" Then pause and wait for their answer. Most of the time they will say yes, but other times they will throw out an objection that you need to be ready to handle. Objections at this point are things like: We like you but we have two other agents to interview, or we want to list, but the house needs a few renovations, or we want to list with you but we are afraid of *not* finding the right house after we sell. We will go over these objections later, but you need to be ready for these in an empathetic and helpful way. For example, if they want to paint a room first, I will say no problem, can I give you my painter's number so they can take care of you? And why don't we do the paperwork now and postdate the listing for two weeks to give everyone the time to get their work done. This works almost every time, and you will walk out with an assigned listing. If you don't solve this objection and say ok. call me when the room is painted, you will most likely lose the listing because the sellers will tell all their friends they are selling, and all of their friends will recommend they meet with a different realtor.

Forms and detail. Once the seller has agreed to list with you, make sure all your forms are ready to go and with you. Do not be an amateur and not have the right forms with you when the seller is ready to list. When the seller is filling out the paperwork, make sure you also have a client connect sheet ready to go for the other party to be filling out at the same time. This sheet lets the seller fill out all of the information about themselves. Your goal is to get things like contact information, birthdays, anniversaries, pets' names or anything else that can give you an opportunity to add to your database to personalize your content to them. The client will appreciate how much you care and will fill out almost anything you give them. After all the paperwork is done make sure you discuss the small things like sign location, keys, or anything else so there are no misunderstandings. Congratulations, you have just perfected the skill of the listing presentation.

Buyer's Presentation 101

If someone were to call you today and say, "I want to buy a house right now," what would you do? If you are like most agents, or me when I started my career, you would say, "Great! Let's start looking," and this would be the wrong answer. Early in my career I thought the more properties I showed the better the experience would be for everyone. What I learned was the more properties I showed the *less* enjoyable the experience was. The buyers would get decision fatigue, I would get frustrated, and even if we did write an offer, it often fell apart anyway. I was not a professional yet, and both my buyers and I paid for it. If you feel stuck, or every buyer seems difficult and hard to close, then we probably need to examine your buyer presentation.

Buyer's presentations are often overlooked in real estate, and they should not be. I would argue that a buyer presentation is just as important as a listing presentation. When done correctly, these presentations will make your clients happier, and the transactions will take less time.

The purpose of a buyer presentation is to build relationships, set expectations, and prove your value. Think of buyer presentations as viewing a map before you go on a road trip. Most buyers don't know what they don't know. Many of them watch HGTV and assume that the buying process consists of one day of viewing a few perfect houses followed by a free lunch to decide which one to buy.

In addition to having unrealistic expectations, buyers often feel stressed, overwhelmed, and scared of making a mistake. So how do we as salespeople create a positive and successful buying experience for our clients? One way is to have an awesome buyer's presentation that you use every single time.

Here is how it works:

Get an in-person meeting. Often buyers will be hesitant to meet with you because they just want to see houses immediately. This puts the buyers in control and will make the process take longer and be more difficult for everyone, so an in-person meeting is the essential first step.

Ask if you can take them for coffee. Let them know it will be maximum forty-five minutes and stress how important it is that you get to know them a little bit, so that you can help them find the best house possible. In my experience, they will rarely turn you down. Also, if they are willing to meet with you, it is unlikely they will go with another realtor.

Meet them at a local coffee shop in the area where you work. This is a strategic move so that you can develop a reputation in the area for being a kind, hard-working, and busy agent. Go to the same coffee shop so that the staff will come to know you and be likely to give you a call when they want to buy or sell. Always treat the barista well!

Now that you have bought a coffee for your clients, you can dive into your presentation. The first part of the presentation will put your listening skills in play by asking lots of great questions. Tell them how excited you are for them and ask what the perfect house for them would look like. Listen carefully and have a notebook with you to take notes as they are talking. They will be excited to talk about their hopes and dreams and remember, at this point it is just that: hopes and dreams. Very often with new buyers, they will tell you they want one thing, but will end up buying something else. Ask them things like: What is your favourite location? Does a backyard matter? Do you entertain? Do you work from home? Do you commute? Does the school catchment matter? Do you like to cook? Where do you see yourself in five years? Do you need a mortgage helper? Listening to their answers builds trust. Remember that people don't care how much you know until they know how much you care.

After letting them talk about their hopes and dreams, the next step is to talk about the process. This is where I ask how familiar they are with the whole process of buying a property. Regardless of what they say, you need to communicate that things are always changing, and that you want them to know exactly how the process works so you can work together as a team.

Next, I talk about the actual buyer's tour, which I will go into in more detail later in the chapter. At this stage, I tell them that for the first tour, I will pick the homes and they are not allowed to buy anything, as we are simply on a "buyer education tour." I tell them that pictures are often deceiving, so it is important to walk through and get a feel for each property.

Then I tell them about the next step in the process, which I call "getting serious." This is where you tell them about next steps once they find an 80 percent house, so they fully understand what it looks like to write an offer. I tell them about the forms required, how an offer works, and how I protect them with contingencies. The buyer education presentation should have all of the forms for an offer included at the back for them to read on their own time. Giving more information only builds more trust. During this time, I bring up the closing techniques we discussed earlier. I tell my buyers that it is not worth losing a great home over a certain threshold of money, so I tell them to prepare themselves for my "reduce to the ridiculous" closing technique. If you bring this up now, when you use it later, everyone will laugh. If you try closing a buyer or seller with the "reduce to the ridiculous close" without preparing them for it, it will come off as pushy and I promise it will not work.

Next, I talk about negotiation. I explain that it is best for the buyer and seller to work together for a fair price and that our goal is to have both parties happy to work together. We also need to explain how writing an offer does not mean they are committed. Sometimes the thought of writing an offer is overwhelming, so again we need to explain the process. Our customers need to know that after the offer is written comes the inspection, and if this goes badly, they can back out of the deal. This is also when I prepare them for what may happen in an inspection and what sorts of things are deal breakers and what are things we can work with. Preparing the buyer for potential scenarios will stop the deal from falling apart over a furnace that needs to be replaced.

The next thing to bring up is timelines. Remember the theme of a buyer's presentation is to manage client expectations. Often buyers will not understand what a realistic timeline looks like. Your goal is to educate them on timelines, so they can plan accordingly. Let them know that the buyers' education tour will be complete seven days from now. The "getting serious" tours to find a house takes one to three weeks. Negotiating and getting an offer accepted takes two days. Contingencies and terms of a contract take two weeks. On average, it can take four to eight weeks to closing after all contingencies are met. If you do the math from today to moving in, you are looking at roughly two and a half to three and a half months. When buyers learn the timeline, they will put pressure on themselves to get moving so that you won't have to.

The next thing I do is anticipate and handle future objections, which we have already dealt with in-depth. You always want to handle objections like cold feet/buyer's remorse before they happen. To date, I have not had a single person back out of a deal because of cold feet or buyer's remorse because I always prepare them for it in advance.

Now it is time to talk about qualifying. Set your buyer up for success by finding out what they can afford. Too many realtors hop in their cars with unqualified buyers, show twenty houses, write an offer on one of them, only to have it fall apart because of financing. In this case, time is wasted, and no one is happy. Early in my career I fell for this. I was too scared to ask the hard questions at the beginning, so I would work hundreds of hours only to lose more deals than I care to admit. A well-prepared and executed buyer's presentation avoids all of this. Ask your buyers if they have been pre-qualified and if they have met with a banker or mortgage broker. If they say yes, you need to get the contact information for their finance person so that you can personally follow up with them. At this point, I always recommend getting a second opinion. I want them working with a bank or mortgage broker that I know and trust so I can be sure the client is getting professional service. I am not willing to risk a transaction going wrong because the client chose a bad mortgage broker. It is also wise to ask for their income, if they have any debts, and if their credit is good. At this point, I will often tell them to hold off getting a new car until they move into their new home. I once had clients find the perfect house that was within their budget.

When we went for the second viewing, they suddenly had a fancy new car. I asked how they bought it, and they said they got such a good interest rate, they couldn't say no. Unfortunately, that car loan ended up costing them their dream home, and we had to start over looking at houses well below the original budget.

Bring them into your sphere of influence. By the end of the meeting, you need to make sure you have demonstrated your competency and the value you bring them. A great way to do this is by giving them contacts within your sphere. Your sphere of influence includes anyone who can help them with the transaction: mortgage broker, home inspector, lawyer or attorney, insurance company, appraiser, handyman, and others. The more contacts you have, the more your clients will appreciate your experience and trust you for their future real estate needs. A bonus is that referring clients to your sphere of influence plays double duty because those contacts will in turn refer you to people in their spheres.

Remember to stick to your promise that the meeting will not take more than forty-five minutes. At the end of the meeting, make sure a time is set for the buyer's education tour. If they have not been qualified yet, make sure you leave enough time for a mortgage broker to give them a quick idea of the budget before you go out. Make sure to leave them your buyer's tour book to go through after the meeting, which will include everything you have discussed, all the forms for writing an offer, testimonials of your service, an overview of the process, tips to finding the right house, and more. A copy of this can be found in the www.elevatecoachingco.com Courses page.

You are now prepared for the buyer's tour!

Buyer's Tours

A couple of years ago, a "house-hunter" TV show contacted me, asking if I had sold a certain type of house in the last three years.

They wanted to use it as a "prop" for the buyer-actors they had hired for an episode. I was flabbergasted at how fake the house hunting show actually was. Unfortunately for realtors in the real world, millions of people watch these shows and think that a day in the life of a realtor involves showing a buyer three homes, going for a fancy lunch where the buyer chooses which of the three to buy, followed by a champagne celebration. The reality is that buyer's tours involve a whole lot more work. In my opinion, not enough is taught in our industry about how to make these tours as successful as possible.

When I first started in real estate, my goal was to get buyers in my truck and show them as many properties as possible. I thought that the more homes I showed and the harder I worked, the more I would sell. But the opposite started to happen. Suddenly buyers were taking up all of my time and few of them actually made decisions to purchase. I would show a buyer fifty or more homes only to see them become unhappy and stressed when they finally made a decision. There had to be a better way.

Fortunately, there is. Let's dive into some simple ground rules for a successful buyer's tour.

Ensure the buyers you are taking out are qualified. Do not take out buyers if you don't know what they can afford. My only exception to this rule is when I use my open house soft-closing technique. When I meet brand new people in an open house, I offer them a zero-obligation tour of six homes in the area to help educate them about the area they are wanting to move into. In fact, I tell the potential buyers they are not even allowed to buy a house. But other than that, it is a hard and fast rule to know what your buyers can afford before you take them on a tour.

Do not do a buyer's tour until you have done a buyer's presentation. The foundation of trust will have already been laid in that presentation and you will have set the "win-win" tone of your relationship, making it clear from the beginning that it is not about you trying to talk them into buying a house.

Never show more than six houses at a time and four is preferred. It is vital that you choose at least half the homes on the tour. You are the professional and want to demonstrate that you have listened to them and have chosen homes that you believe fit with their wants and needs. Six homes is the limit because of something called decision fatigue. Studies have been done showing that if you give someone the choice between picking red or blue, they will make a decision quickly, and their overall satisfaction will generally be high. If you give the same person sixty different colours and ask them to pick their favourite, they will be paralyzed by indecision, and when they finally do make a choice, they will be less happy than if they only had two choices. If you show your clients twelve houses during one tour, they will be exhausted and overwhelmed with the differences between each home. However, if you show them four to six houses, they will have a much easier time making a decision and their overall satisfaction with the process will be much higher.

The first tour is for educational purposes only. I always tell my buyers that I will not allow them to buy a house on the first trip out. This has turned out to be a very effective way to end up with the clients closing themselves. What happens when you tell a human they are not allowed to do something? That's right. They want to do it. Tell someone not to think of a pink elephant, and that's all they can think about. My sincere intention is that the first tour will be for "buyer education" only, but very often we get to the end of the tour, and my clients will say some version of the following: "I know we are breaking the rules, but we really want to buy this home." If this happens, of course I write up the offer!

Your buyers must drive with you in your car. When buyers are in your car, you have the chance to learn about their lives and deepen your trust relationship. You can point out things that they might not know about the area as you drive, which demonstrates your competence in a natural way. I like to call my buyer's tours "shopping with friends." Buy them coffees, have water in the car along with extra clipboards so everyone can participate in rating each home on the three main factors: price, location, and floor plan. I give each of my buyers a clipboard with the properties on it, and I ask them to rate every property out of ten for the layout, price, and location. These are the three main factors when deciding on a home, so I let them figure out what matters most to them. This is much less intimidating than me asking what they thought of every property. It's a fun game, and they are closing themselves instead of me being a pushy salesperson.

Make it a fun and positive experience. After you have viewed a home and are driving together to the next one, you have a chance to talk to them about how they have rated the home on the three key factors. If they are in their own vehicle, you will not be able to pick up on their thoughts, opinions, or learn more about their exact needs.

If at any point on the tour, your buyers say they want to buy a house, stop the tour immediately and drive to the office to prepare the offer. This might seem odd, but if they have closed themselves or come to a decision, then you need to get on board. There is an internal clock that every buyer has when they make a decision. If you take too long to get the offer written and negotiated, the buyers will start thinking of a million reasons not to buy that house. After all the old saying is very true—"time kills deals."

Additional Tips for Elevating your Sales Skills: Build Core Connections

Building connections is an underrated sales skill. As realtors, the more people who know, like, and trust us, the more homes we will sell. In today's world, a savvy realtor will be service-orientated and will constantly be making far more deposits than withdrawals in the relationship bank. You want to be the person a client calls when they need a referral for anything. I even have clients contacting me to ask who I would recommend they buy a car from! Our job is to be connecters: the bridge between all parties.

Core connections are anything that brings value to a real estate transaction. Think about all the possible referrals a buyer or seller will need during a sale. If a seller's house is in rough shape and needs a small renovation before listing, they will potentially need a plumber, painter, flooring company, kitchen and bathroom company, finish carpenter, HVAC person, and more. If you can provide the client with trusted contacts in these areas, you have just deposited value into the relationship bank.

If you are strategic with your connections, every one of them can eventually become a buyer or a seller, with you as their realtor. If you give that plumber several referrals every year, who do you think they will use to sell their home?

A reasonable goal is to have fifty to one hundred connections related to the purchase and sale of a home. Having this many core connections has the potential to explode your sales volume. Not only will you have your regular database, you will have an additional fifty to one hundred people who will use you and refer you on a regular basis. The more referrals you give them, the more you get back. Mutual referrals among your core connections creates mutually beneficial relationships.

Here is a guide to building a core connections list:

1. First, make an Excel spreadsheet listing all the services required in a real estate transaction. This is everything from mortgage brokers, to stagers, to carpenters, to moving companies. Your minimum goal should be fifty, one hundred is optimal. If you have been a realtor for many years, you may already know or have a connection with many of these

businesses. If you are new, you will be starting from scratch building new relationships. These core connections need to be treated in a similar way as your database: connecting with them once a month, sending them birthday cards, market updates and swag.

2. When this list of core connections is finished, it should be saved in two formats. The first format is to use in your advertising package when you meet clients for your listing or buyer's presentations. You can call this your core connections list. There is an example at www.elevatecoachingco. com. The second format is for your database connection. Essentially, this list of core connections becomes another arm of your database. If you have forty businesses on your core connections list, and your database is one hundred families, you now have one hundred forty people in your database.

3. Once you have the businesses organized, you need to take another step: define the relationship with each contact. Your contact must have two qualities if you are going to refer them to your clients. First, they must be good at what they do and do it for a reasonable price. If you refer your seller to a painter, and they are bad or overpriced, it will reflect poorly on you. Second, they must be loyal to you as a realtor. Remember this is a mutually beneficial relationship. Spend your time building relationships with people who will elevate your business. For example, I had a painter who I referred a lot of work to and in return, he used me as his realtor. Then his brother got his real estate license and became his new agent, which meant I would no longer be getting referrals in return. I found another good quality painter who would use me as his realtor, so I could keep the referral cycle going. This perhaps sounds a bit cutthroat,

but it's important to your business that these are mutually beneficial, win-win relationships.

In order to define the relationship with your core connections, you must meet face to face with every person on your list. You need to have a very direct conversation to define the relationship, making it clear that you will be loyal to each other's business.

Let's pretend we are talking to Carl the carpenter at a meeting at your local coffee shop. Always start with questions about how he is, how his family is, and how his business is going to make sure you have a strong foundation. Remember, relationships matter! Next, you are going to say something like this: "Carl, I asked you for coffee because I want to talk to you about my core connection list. As you know, I am a local realtor, and I represent a lot of families buying and selling in the area. My goal is to provide all my clients with great service and having a skilled carpenter that I can connect them with really matters to me. I have a core connections list that I give to every client and I wanted to see if you would be interested in being on that list, with the understanding that it will be a symbiotic relationship: if I refer you clients, in return, you would be willing to refer me clients. What do you think about that?"

Then you will show Carl a piece of your marketing package that has the list of contacts you give to your clients. Carl the carpenter will see the list and want to be on it. Further, he will see the win-win: that sharing referrals will benefit both of your businesses. I understand that this might seem like an awkward conversation to have, but any business owner you meet with will appreciate it. Carl might say that he's loyal to a different agent personally, but is happy to refer his friends and family to you, or he might say that he's 100 percent in for the mutual referrals. He also might say no altogether, to which you will say, it's no problem, that you will keep him on your list, but you will prioritize the people you have a symbiotic relationship with. Keep the conversation positive, clear, and upfront to avoid any misunderstandings or future complications.

The Math of Core Connections

The path is in the math, so let's see if a core connection list is worth it. Let's assume an average commission of $10,000 and you start a core connection list with forty businesses on it, and all of them are loyal to you. Statistically, 20 percent of your core connections will move every year personally, resulting in eight listings and eight buyers per year for a total of sixteen sales. Next, you should receive at least one referral a year per business, which means an additional forty referrals a year. If you only close 25 percent of those referrals, that means another ten transactions. In total, your core connections will bring your business twenty-six transactions per year. That's an extra $260,000 in gross commissions. With this kind of math, how can you not develop a core connection list?

Marketing

Marketing is like riding a bike: when you stop pedalling, you fall over. In sales, we need to be top of mind when people are thinking of buying or selling or we will miss out. Many business people will argue that marketing is even more important than sales. My goal isn't to prove one over the other, but rather to give you some basic principles of marketing in real estate.

If you have a well-run business, great marketing is like pouring gasoline on the fire. I once had an agent working for me who sold over 175 homes per year. In addition to being a talented agent, she was also an expert at marketing. Everywhere you would drive in town, you would see her face on a billboard; it was impossible to drive anywhere in our city without seeing her face. She became a household name because of her top-of-mind advertising, and this helped drive her sales.

The best part about real estate is that we can be very creative with our marketing dollars. Some agents do it for free with content on YouTube or social media, while others spend money on billboards, TV, or radio. You can be as unique as you want to be. I have done newspaper ads, tag marketing, radio commercials, bus benches, funnel sites, and sponsored countless community events. Before you spend time and money marketing, I want to give you a few tips to help you build a marketing plan that works for you.

Target Audience

You need to know who your audience is and what message you want to send them. I firmly believe that you can get into any market you want to: modular homes, commercial, new construction, acreages, luxury homes, etc., but you need to choose your niche. Pick the type of market that matches your personality and lifestyle. If you are a middle-class person living in suburbia, then you should target that market. If you love horses and grew up on a ranch, then ranch lands might be your target. I grew up on a job site and love new construction and land development, so by default that has been a large part of my target market. I love finding great pieces of land that I can bring to developers. I can talk shop with any builder or developer because it has been my world for most of my life. Target a market that you have experience with.

Market to your Database

Put the contacts from your database into google maps and see where the pins end up. This is a good indication of where you should target your marketing dollars. If your database is mostly located on one side of town, why would you advertise anywhere else? We know that our database is our best source of business, so we want them to see us as much as possible. I have billboards and bus benches, and I sponsor community events in the area where most of my potential clients are. Doing this will keep you top of mind and help you dominate that area.

Have a Plan

You will be more successful if you have a plan, and it is much simpler than you think. A good plan includes a yearly budget for advertising, your target market, the types of advertising you will try, your message, and how you will measure the effectiveness of your advertising after one year.

Whatever plan you implement, remember that *you* are the product. You need to sell yourself and be top of mind when people need a real estate agent. Whether you are a team leader or solo agent, the goal of marketing is for people to get to know who you are, so they think of you when they decide to buy or sell. We can do this in two ways: ego marketing (or self-marketing) and product marketing. Both work well and both have their target markets.

Ego Marketing

Ego marketing is all about promoting yourself as loudly as possible. One example is the billboards we see everywhere: a giant picture of someone with a smiling face, a list of awards they've won, a cheesy slogan and a phone number. Realtors do this so often that the picture doesn't even have to say, "real estate" and the public still knows they are a realtor.

Ego marketing can take many forms. I used to market on the radio and had impressive results. I suddenly had a lot of doctors calling me to sell their homes, and I couldn't figure out why. Then I realized that my radio ads were on a local station that played in every doctor's office in town, and over time, my name was the one they thought of when they decided to buy or sell property.

Whatever method of ego marketing you choose, remember the following tips:

1. **Consistency is Key**

   Whatever advertising route you choose, stick to it. A good rule of thumb is to commit to something for a year and then evaluate its effectiveness. Too many realtors try a newspaper ad one week, a bus bench the next, then tag marketing the next. The consumer must see your name over and over for it to sink in. Your branding also needs to be consistent. Your billboard should look the same as your website, your business card, and your bus bench.

2. **Keep it Simple**

   Keep your name large and include a couple of basic stats. This is not the time to have testimonials or intricate pictures in the background. The best branding is simple and has lots of space. Ego marketing is all about name recognition. Most consumers have a short attention span and won't read the details anyway. If a consumer remembers your name, in one minute they can look you up on the internet and learn all about you.

3. **Product Marketing**

   Product marketing can also be very effective. With product marketing, you can take a product like a nice listing you have and advertise it to gain self-recognition. This is a little less flashy and does the same trick, plus your sellers will be very happy at how much you are promoting their property. In certain markets, like land development or luxury homes, you will have a better chance at gaining market share from product promotion than from ego marketing. Many times, more traffic will be driven to your website through ego marketing because potential clients are looking for the product you are advertising.

Conclusion

Back in 2008, I set about acquiring the sales skills I needed to become the successful real estate agent I wanted to be. I hope that you will take the practical tips and hard-earned lessons I have shared in this chapter and put them into practice. I know from experience that when you do, you will see your business grow and thrive consistently in any market.

Chapter 8: Next Level Sales—How to Massively Increase Transactions

Go Hunting for Sales

Find the deal, and the money will follow. Burn this into your memory if you want to take your sales to the next level. Let me explain what I mean. If you knew of an amazing deal on a property where a buyer could make over $100,000 in six months, would it be hard for you to find a buyer for this property? Of course not! When you find a great deal, a buyer will always follow. We often have it backwards in our industry. We target a buyer first, then we try to find them a property. What if you hunted for deals and then brought them to buyers? This is another activity I love because the playing field is completely even. It doesn't matter if you are young, old, experienced, or brand new, if you find a great deal, you will get a buyer. If I am ever short on my goals for the month, I always go hunting for deals. Once I find an opportunity, I simply pick up the phone and call buyers until I find someone who wants to buy it. This is a fun activity and a great way to connect with your database and meet all the movers and shakers in your area. You know who I mean: the entrepreneurs who are always open to new opportunities. These will be builders, renovators, developers, flippers, and investors—all people you want to be developing relationships with!

I had a new agent who started working for me a few years ago who adopted this principal right away. He was having trouble getting started, but he was out looking for good pieces of land constantly so he could call a developer or builder to make a deal. I told him he was in over his head and that he should stick to his database and open houses. He informed me that he was doing open houses and connecting with his database, but he still had time to go "hunting." I felt very proud to be a mentor in his life because this guy was on the right track. A few months later, he informed me that he found a seller who wanted to sell a huge piece of developable property in our area, and all he needed to do was get a buyer. It didn't take him long to find a buyer, and he put together the biggest deal our office saw that year. He sold a property for over $56 million dollars and received a commission of approximately $550,000 dollars. Did I mention that he was a brand-new real estate agent? Even new realtors can put together huge deals if they go hunting for them.

Every market and location will have its own nuances, but I want to give you a few tips about hunting for deals. Your job is to be able to navigate your market and be creative. This means you need to get to know your area better than anyone else. You need to know what the city is planning in the future and what direction your town is headed. You should know of all the upcoming infrastructure projects planned, including knowledge of roads, transit, planned communities, density changes, and so on. You should always be talking to city planners and attending zoning meetings if possible. All municipalities allow for community members to attend council meetings, so you should put this in your schedule, and attend every meeting possible. You want to get to know what builders and developers are looking for so that you can be the one to bring them opportunities.

This can be as simple or as complex as you want it to be. On the simple side, you can find a run-down property that needs some sweat equity and present it to young buyers. On the complex side, you can get three or four neighbours together that have old homes with big yards in an area that the municipality has rezoned for apartments. If you can get a few neighbours to sign an agreement with you, then you can figure out how many apartments can be built and then go looking for developers who build apartments. One of my favourite things to do is find larger properties that can be broken up into smaller single-family lots and bring them to a builder. Once, I found a one-acre parcel in a community of small lot homes that had not been developed yet. I built a relationship with the seller and told them I could reach out to developers on their behalf to get them the most money possible, and then I could help them relocate after they got a great deal on their home. They agreed, so I made a plan and started reaching out to the movers and shakers in town. Within twenty-four hours, I had a buyer for the property and made a deal with him that I would get all the listings for the twelve new lots after he finished the subdivision. When the dust settled, I got two sales on the original property (the buy and sell), plus another sale for the owners who had to move, and twelve sales after the developer took the one acre and split it into twelve lots. By going hunting and finding a good deal, I secured myself fifteen transactions from one property. Hunting for sales is one way to take your sales to the next level. If you can add fifteen sales every year by hunting and add that to the consistent sales from your database and open houses, you will be in the top percentage of realtors in North America. The best part about hunting is that it is a lot more fun than cold-calling or door-knocking!

One important thing to note when bringing deals to the movers and shakers in your community is that you must present a plan. Calling and saying you have found a good deal looks unprofessional. Have a plan in writing before you present it. For example, if you find a potential renovation and flip home, you need to do the math before presenting it to buyers. Your plan would include the purchase price (for example $100,000), the cost of required renovations ($50,000), the value after renovations ($200,000), and the potential profit ($50,000). Your plan will go into greater detail and be laid out nicely. It should have all the costs to purchase and sell as well as a detailed list of all the renovations required and the cost of each. For something like a property amalgamation with apartments, you should get the expected density from a city planner and have that on your presentation as well. For example, let's say you get three homes together that equal one acre, and you know that the city allows for apartments in that area as long as it is on a one-acre site. You find out that the city will allow eighty-five apartments on a one-acre site and now you can put together a presentation and start calling developers. If you do the deal right, you should be able to get the listings for the eighty-five apartments when they are ready, plus the three homes from the original deal. Quite clearly, hunting for deals will take your sales to the next level.

Investing in Real Estate

Investing is real estate is an untapped superpower for realtors and is another way to take your sales to the next level. In today's world, agents will do anything for residual income or a downline, but for some reason, they won't invest in real estate. Investing in real estate is one of the easiest ways to increase your sales and give you residual income. For years, I have had a goal of increasing my active income (selling houses) per hour and passive income (residual income) per hour. For example, if I make $200,000 a year selling houses and I work two thousand hours that means that my active income is $100 per hour. If I have two rental properties, and they pay down $50,000 per year in principle, I divide that by two thousand hours to find my passive income of $25 per hour. Combined, my gross income for the year is $125 per hour. Selling and investing is a symbiotic relationship for a realtor, and we should take advantage of it. When a realtor buys a rental house for themselves, they get paid commission (active income) to buy the property that will now bring you residual income through principal repayment. So if you want to get more sales, then you need to become your own client. When you are your own client, both your active income and passive income will increase.

Let's say you are hunting for a deal, and you come across two cheap properties that qualify as renovation and flip or renovation and hold projects. You call your list of movers and shakers and none of them want to move forward. This just may be the opportunity for you to become your own client to increase both your active and passive income. The path is always in the math, so here is how it looks: let's say the homes are $200,000 each and both require $100,000 in renovations, but they will be worth $350,000 when completed, and the average commission per sale is $10,000. With these numbers, when you buy the two homes and sell them in the same year, you create four sales for a total of $40,000 in gross commission (or $20 per hour if you work two thousand hours per year). Another benefit to your business when you become your own client is that you can call your core connections to do the renovations, which will increase your chance at getting referrals. After the sale of these renovated homes, you will have made a profit of $50,000 per home for a total of $100,000 of passive income. You have now increased your passive income to $50 per hour and your active income to $20 per hour and your yearly per hour income just jumped to $70.

If you set a goal to "buy and flip" or "buy and keep" at least one property per year, you will greatly increase your sales. Another added value of becoming your own client is that you will become a savvy investor and your knowledge in this area will bring so much value to your future clients.

Chapter 9: Essential Knowledge

Buyer's Market and Seller's Market—MOI

Professional realtors need to be market experts. We need to know all the different market conditions and how they affect our buyers and sellers. When a member of the public asks us the classic question, "How is the market?" we need to be ready. Answering this question by talking about the market as a buyer's market, a seller's market, or a balanced market, gives us the opportunity to demonstrate knowledge in such a natural way. At the beginning of every month in my sales meeting, I always ask the newest realtor if it's a buyer's market or a seller's market. This usually catches them off guard, and they go red in the face. I know it's a little mean because they are new to the industry, but I want them to understand the importance of knowing the market. The real estate course focuses more on teaching new realtors how to stay out of real estate jail than it does about how to sell homes or be experts in the market. My goal is always to help realtors have a basic understanding of how our real estate cycle works so they can give the best advice possible to their clients.

The first step to being able to give good advice to any client is understating the type of market we are working in. It is vital for us to know what market presents a good time to downsize or upsize or buy a rental. In calculating a buyer's market and a seller's market, we are working with three variables: unit sales, inventory, and time. The first is unit sales, or the number of sales that happen in one month in the marketplace you're working in. The second variable is inventory, or the number of homes actively for sale at any given time. The last variable is time. We try to figure out how long it will take for all of the active inventory to be sold if no more properties hit the market. This is calculated in months of inventory or MOI. Say there are one hundred sales every month, and there are five hundred homes for sale. This means it would take five months for all the homes to sell if no other homes got listed. Therefore, there would be five months of inventory (MOI). After we figure this out, we need to know the parameters of the different markets. A seller's market is zero to five MOI, a balanced market is five to eight MOI, and a buyer's market is eight plus MOI.

Seller's Market

A seller's market is zero to five MOI, which means in five or less months, all the homes on the market will be sold if nothing new hits the market. The conditions of a seller's markets become more extreme as you move from five MOI to zero MOI. The first thing you will notice in a seller's market is that prices will be rising, which happens because there is more demand than there is supply. The next thing you will notice in a seller's market is the speed of decision-making. Since inventory is low, buyers won't have a lot of choice, so they will make decisions very quickly. The terms of the offer will favour the seller as buyers want to make an attractive offer so that the seller accepts. The buyer will have very few contingencies or conditions in their offer, and they will try to do whatever the seller asks. Everything works in favour of the seller: they get to dictate the terms, price, and timing. The closer you get to zero months of inventory; the faster prices rise and the more you will see multiple offers on the same property. I have worked some extreme seller's markets where over fifty buyers submitted an offer on one property. It is important to know how to give buyers good advice in a seller's market. It is a great time for new construction, flipping houses, selling rentals, buying vacation homes, or downsizing from an expensive property to a cheaper one. On the other hand, a seller's market is bad for first-time buyers, people buying more expensive houses, or those buying rentals. Seller's markets can be thrilling and fast paced, but for the most part, I hate them. Buyers are driven by the fear of missing out and therefore make quick and often bad decisions. Buyers will forgo home inspections and won't do the proper research to make sure they are buying a good property. It is also hard to schedule appointments for viewings because everything is immediate: if a house hits the market in the afternoon, then you better be out that evening ready to write an offer, so you don't miss out.

Balanced Market

A balanced market is five to eight months of inventory. This is my favourite market. Both buyers and seller are treated fairly, and all parties have reasonable amounts of time to make wise decisions. The market is in harmony, and the flow of sales is very stable. If a home is priced right, it will sell and if it is overpriced it won't sell. In a balanced market, realtors with systems and a database will really excel. In this market you are in control of scheduling your day, and clients will listen to your advice. A balanced market gives you time to build relationships and demonstrate your value. A balanced market is a safe time to resume all market activities, whether you are a first-time buyer or a savvy investor.

Buyer's Market

A buyer's market is eight or more MOI, and it is the market where people think the sky is falling. A buyer's market has some fundamental similarities with a balanced market, like a drop in prices and increased decision time. But a buyer's market has a twist: everyone becomes pessimistic, including buyers, even though the market favours them, and they get to dictate all the terms of the offer. They get to decide price, contingencies, timing, and include extra items they might want in a property. The buyer has time to do the proper due diligence and rarely makes a mistake when buying a home. The buyer also has lots of choice and no competition from other buyers. A buyer's market is perfect for first-time buyers, land developers, investors and people who want to upgrade their home. Developers are usually the biggest winners because they can buy development properties at good prices and since it takes a few years to complete the project, the houses are ready to sell when the market shifts back to a seller's market.

It is really important to learn how to navigate a buyer's market. Consumers are more emotional during this market, and it shows up in poor decision-making. We all know that we should buy low and sell high, yet so many people buy high and sell low. People are motivated by the fear of loss, and we don't want to do anything that the crowd doesn't do. When prices drop, the consumer thinks it will keep dropping forever, so they are unwilling to buy at a good deal, thinking the price will keep falling. It's the syndrome of not wanting to catch the falling knife. The conditions favour buyers, yet they are hesitant to buy anything. When a buyer has no reason to buy and lots of choice, they usually will not make a decision causing a buyer's market to snowball.

Early in my career, I was working in a very slow buyer's market, so I thought I would be proactive. I knew it was the best time for first-time buyers to be buying, so I decided to run a first-time buyer's seminar to help educate them and turn them into buyers. It was the perfect time for them to buy, and I had lots of time to sell them homes. I sent out invites to everyone in my market, I bought food and drinks, I even got a builder to let me host it in a new house that was vacant. Guess how many people showed up for my amazing event with tons of value? Zero. Not a single person showed up! Looking back now, anyone who had bought at that time would have made a lot of money, but no one was willing to be the first to buy.

Many realtors can succeed in a seller's market or a balanced market, but a buyer's market will crush them. As the saying goes, a rising tide floats all boats but when the tide goes out, we find out who was swimming naked. The best way to sell in a buyer's market is through education and hunting good deals. In this market, a good realtor can demonstrate value and add clients for life. The money is always made when you buy the property not when you sell it. When you sell a property, you are just realizing the gain from a good purchase. Therefore, if I can find my clients great deals in a buyer's market, they will be clients for life when I help make them a lot of money. Another great thing about a buyer's market is the opportunity you have to educate your clients and build relationships. When the pressure of a frenzied seller's market isn't there, you can spend valuable time going to viewings in the same vehicle with your clients and really getting to know them. It is such an honour to be part of our clients' lives during major life changes, which is when moves happen: getting married, having their first child, becoming empty nesters, retiring, and even some sadder times like divorce or the death of a spouse. In a buyer's market, we have an opportunity to really appreciate and develop the relationships we get to build with our fellow humans. I love this part of being a realtor.

A buyer's market also allows me to find and buy properties at great deals for my own real estate portfolio. Remember, a realtor's greatest client should be themselves. The last thing I love about a buyer's market is that there is less competition from other realtors. During this market, many realtors will become pessimistic or even give up their license. If my only competition is a sad realtor with a negative outlook on the market, then I will beat them every time. Sales is about energy, skill, and optimism. I hope I have convinced you of the many reasons you should love a buyer's market.

The Laws of Real Estate: Location and Timing

We have all heard that the three laws of real estate are location, location, location. This is a great slogan, but it is not the whole truth. Yes, location matters and should be a major factor in any decision, but we also need to consider timing. As trained and knowledgeable professionals, we need to teach our clients that the market is cyclical. I understand that if you step back and take a fifty-year approach, then value does increase on a straight line, but we don't buy and sell real estate with fifty years in mind.

There are so many scenarios where timing really matters. I have seen beautiful projects in the best locations go broke because the market crashed. The developer considered all the right things and built a great product but still lost everything. I have also seen scenarios where someone built the ugliest house in a terrible neighbourhood and still made a ton of money when he shouldn't have made a dime; they got lucky because they timed the market perfectly. We see this in house flipping all the time. A non-sophisticated first-time flipper will buy a home and spend the next year renovating the house themselves every weekend and then sell it for a huge profit. Let's use $80,000 dollars as an example of the profit they made. They are so proud of themselves that they quit their job and start flipping full-time. What they don't realize is that they are most likely on the path to losing everything. The first house they flipped probably took too long, and they likely overpaid for at least some of the improvements along the way. Because of the cyclical nature of the market, that same house would have gone up $100,000 over the same amount of time without improvements being made to it. This means that any money they put into the renovation only increased the price by 80 percent of their expenses for making those renos. Let's look at the numbers: say the original house was purchased for $500,000. After one year with good market timing, you could have sold the house for $600,000 without doing anything to it. But the first-time renovator bought the house for $500,000 and put $80,000 into it for a total price of $580,000. After the improvements, they sold the house for $660,000. The first-time renovator only sees the profit they made but does not understand the bigger picture of good market timing. They look at the $80,000 profit, when in reality they lost $20,000 (if the market stayed even). All the profit was made on the timing of the market. It is hard to watch when this person doesn't listen to your advice and learns the hard way when they lose a lot of money on their next flip because of a downturn in the market. Our job as professional realtors is to always consider the timing of the market when giving advice to clients.

Boom, Bust, Recovery

The market has three cycles: boom, bust, and recovery. There are many very detailed books written on this subject, but I want to give you the basics. Realtors do not need to be economists, but they need to have a basic understanding of how the market cycle works. The first thing you need to know is that "cycle" means the process repeats itself over and over. When the market is booming, we think it will last forever and when it busts, we think it will be bad forever. This is not true. The market will continue on the same cycle it was on for my grandparents and the same cycle it will be on for my grandkids. Understanding this is what can keep you level-headed, optimistic, and wise about your sales. If you know that the market will crash, then it will not surprise you when it does. A great saying that will help you weather the ups and downs of the market goes like this: when it's good, it's never as good as you think it is, and when it's bad, it's never as bad as you think it is.

The cycles are typically seven to ten years but can vary depending on a lot of different factors. My first market crash was the 2008 financial meltdown. At that time, it was overwhelming, and I thought it would last forever. I felt like the sky was falling and thought my sales career was over. I was just starting out and had never experienced a market crash, so I was overly emotional. Looking back, I probably gave a lot of bad advice to my clients at that time. Bad advice would be telling your clients they better sell before it gets worse rather than looking at buying opportunities because homes are cheap right now. Another thing I did not do was to save my money in the good times. When the market was good, I thought it would be good forever, so I spent my money as if the good times would keep on rolling. If you learn the cycles and how to navigate them, you will be a wise source of great advice for your clients, and you will save yourself a lot of financial stress.

The Boom

A booming market can be very fun, and it is easy to get caught up in it. The boom is the first part of a market cycle. In a booming market, everyone is making money. Properties are selling for high prices; seller's equity is increasing, so they can buy bigger homes and people ask zero questions about your commission.

Builders, developers, and home flippers are selling for record profits and are willing to speculate on new properties. You will find that as a salesperson, you will have few customer objections to handle. Everyone wants to buy or sell because they don't want to miss out, and we are making commissions at every turn.

A booming market has some key indicators that you need to be aware of: low inventory, low vacancy, high migration, and interest rates. If you have a lot of people moving into an area, and there is not a lot of inventory, then the simple law of supply and demand comes into play and prices will rise. If you pair this will low interest rates and easy access to financing, then you will experience the thrill of a booming market. As a prudent realtor, you need to be monitoring these conditions on a regular basis because indicators are always changing. You will notice some things happening over time: builders will start building more homes and therefore inventory will rise. As inventory rises, banks will be a little more timid and will increase interest rates. The vacancy rates of rental homes will also start to rise because many renters will become homeowners in fear of missing out on the rising market. Then, all of a sudden, the market will crash, and many people did not see it coming even though all of the indicators had been pointing towards a changing market. People get a bit blinded by greed and assume that the boom will last forever and are surprised that the taps have been turned off; the boom is over, and the bust part of the market cycle is here.

I have just described myself in 2008. I was so busy working with buyers and sellers that I didn't notice that inventory had been rising in my area. I thought the market would boom forever and wasn't thinking at all about the future. When the market shifted to a bust, I didn't see it coming, and I don't want the same thing to ever happen to you. I want you to see a bust coming a mile away so you can be prepared. It is the best feeling to be prepared for a market crash while everyone around you seems to be surprised and panicked.

The first step to avoid being blindsided by a crash is to be aware that you are in a booming market. You need to let your clients know that it will not last forever and for them not to let the fear of missing out guide their decisions. A booming market is an amazing time to sell expensive properties, vacation properties, out-of-the-box weird properties, or to downsize. If you have clients who own these types of properties, you need to educate them on the booming market and let them know when the right time to sell is. All the hard-to-sell properties and expensive properties will be sold at a premium during this time. Consumers will use their equity boost to buy more properties: vacation properties, rental properties, and everything in-between. This is the worst time in the market to be buying, but this is when everyone *is* buying. During the boom cycle in the market, everyone seems to be ignoring the tried and true principle to "buy low and sell high" because they are fueled by emotion and are not getting good advice (or are ignoring good advice) from their realtor.

The Bust

A market that is going bust is very difficult to navigate. This market is also fueled by emotion for both clients and realtors. A busting market has the same key indicators as a booming market, except the indicators have reversed. Inventory will be high or rising. Interest rates will be high or rising. The net migration will stall or start to drop. There will also be other indicators in every region such as government interference and changing labour markets, but these are typically more minor. In a bust, you will see prices drop, inventory rise, and both buyers and sellers running for the hills. The activity in the market will dry up along with the number of sales. The greed that fuelled the booming market will suddenly disappear and will be replaced by fear.

A busting market is like a snowball. It will start rolling downhill, getting bigger and faster, and everyone is panicking. Fear can be a powerful thing, but when you begin to learn about how the key indicators affect the emotions of your clients, you will be able to stay calm when everyone else thinks the sky is falling. For example, learning the complexity of inventory will really help you navigate a falling market. When the inventory becomes saturated, buyers start taking longer to make decisions. It is a form of decision fatigue: when there are too many choices, the human brain gets overloaded and can't make a decision, and when it does, the overall happiness they feel about that decision diminishes. Think about kids: if you take them for ice-cream and there are fifty choices, it will take them forever to make a decision and after they choose the cookie-dough, they will wish they had chosen the mint chocolate chip. But if they only had the choice between chocolate or strawberry, and there was another kid in line ready to take the last scoop of chocolate, a decision would be made very quickly, and satisfaction will be high. This example is what happens in a market that is crashing. Suddenly, buyers have lots of choice and no pressure, so they take their time making a decision. Then, as they are deciding, they see prices starting to fall, and no one else buying. Then they don't buy anything because other people aren't buying, and the crash has officially started.

A busting market is when prices start to fall and homes stop selling. In 2022 the prices in the market I was working in dropped a whopping 30 percent. I have never seen that in my lifetime, but I was prepared for it and so was my database. What took me by surprise was how many realtors did not see it coming, which meant they weren't preparing their clients for it. Wise agents will be connected to their database and will be informing them about all the key indicators and whether they should consider buying or selling based on the conditions.

So, step one of a bust market is to recognize that you are in one and know that it won't last forever. Then, if you have homes listed, your number one goal is to inform your sellers that the market is about to drop, and they need to sell quickly before it keeps dropping. It is better to drop $20,000 and sell now than it is to drop $5,000 every two weeks and sell six months later for $60,000 less. I will meet in person with every seller and re-inform them about the market cycles and walk out of each meeting with a game plan that always includes dropping the price to sell quickly and then be able to take advantage of the falling market on the buying end.

The second thing you must do is inform your database of the changing market and how they can take advantage of it. For example, this is a good time to prepare all your investors, builders, developers, and first-time buyers that a buying opportunity is coming. The opportunity isn't today, but it will be coming soon, and they should be prepared for it. Your database will love you for this. It demonstrates your skill and knowledge and shows that you are looking out for their best interests. If I was a first-time buyer and my family realtor reached out to me and said, "I think there is a great buying opportunity coming about eight months from now when the market really dips. We can buy near the low and will have lots of choice to find you a great deal," I would feel like that agent had my best interest at heart and wasn't trying to push me into anything. That is the type of realtor we all should want to be.

All markets have great opportunities, you just need to know how to find them and present them to your clients. This is also a good time for land developers to start picking up good deals and banking land for when the market picks up. When I was younger, it always surprised me how local developers suddenly had all this inventory available when the market was booming. What I didn't know is that they understood the boom, bust, and recovery cycle of the market. When the market is at the peak, they become sellers, and at the bottom they become buyers. They do the opposite to what the average consumer does and are rewarded highly for this. Our job as realtors is to work with developers to find good land deals in the bad times and help them sell the homes they build in the good times.

Another important principle for salespeople is to be personally ready for the bust. When the market busts, selling homes can be very hard for a period of time. Even if there are amazing deals, buyers won't buy, or investors won't have access to money anymore so they can't buy even if they wanted to. We need to be prepared in our personal finances in order to endure or even thrive in these slow times. My recommendation is to save your money and take a beautiful long vacation during the slow times in the market. If I was only a realtor, I would pack up and go explore the world for six months. Go backpacking across Europe, take that safari in Africa, or drive your RV across the continent. For most agents, the boom can be overwhelming, and will take up all your time, but the bust will give you your time back, so take advantage of it.

The Recovery

The recovery is the most normal time in the market. It is typically the longest part of the cycle and always follows the bust. A recovery is the reset to the market that is required. Everyone just went through a boom and bust, which is a roller coaster ride with a lot of emotion. The recovery allows everything to get back on track when all of the fundamentals get to a place of equilibrium. The key indicators are the same as the boom or the bust, but they are at average levels: the inventory is not too high or too low, interest rates are typically stable, and migration is on an even trajectory. A recovering market is like "Goldilocks and the Three Bears": not too hot and not to cold—it is just right!

The recovery market is business as usual. It is a safe time for many types of clients. The best deals are typically gone, and everything is bought and sold at a fair price. Any type of person can buy and sell in a safe and stable environment. I like this environment for older clients or families with young kids because the buying and selling process is stress-free and the variables of price and inventory are not changing drastically. All parties have time and space to make a wise decision for their family and emotion is not in control. For builders and developers, it is a safe time to build out their inventory because they know a boom is coming next in the cycle. As a recovery gets closer to a boom you will notice subtle changes like falling inventory and increasing migration. The interest rates will still be favourable because the banks have no idea a boom is on the way, and it will be easy for consumers to have access to financing. Then, without warning, a boom happens, and the cycle market continues its journey of boom, bust, and recovery.

I hope my crash course in understanding the market cycle will help you be proactive and not reactive. I want you to be personally ready for the changing market and for your clients to be ready and well informed. As you go through market cycles in your career, you will only get better at navigating them.

Chapter 10:
Retire Wealthy

This chapter is an essential part of this book and one of my favourite things to talk about. I have learned from so many coaches over the years, and not even one talked about retiring at a granular level. What is the point of learning all of the skills and working really hard for many years if you can't retire wealthy? This job is sincerely one of the hardest in the world. The days are stressful, long, and uncertain. Most employees start January knowing they will have a consistent paycheque for the rest of the year. If they made $80,000 last year, then they will make $80,000 again this year. Not so in real estate. Every year we start at zero on January first. We risk time and money in the pursuit of commissions. I always ask agents why they want to leave their job and start a new career in real estate, and the most common answer is that they want to make more money and have more time for their family. I admire both reasons, but unfortunately too many agents get lost in the journey of real estate and don't end up where they wanted to be.

The harsh reality is that many salespeople don't retire wealthy. Instead, they keep working till the bitter end of their lives, or they have to rely on their spouse's pension. This makes me so sad when I see it because it doesn't have to be this way. I sincerely believe that almost any agent can retire a millionaire as long as they have the right direction and enough time on their side. You don't have to be a gifted salesperson or pinch every penny either. I vividly remember my first year in real estate. I was twenty-one but looked about twelve, and I would run into the older agents in the hallways of my office and the weirdest thing kept happening. They all seemed to have a cheap cup of coffee in their hand and would give me the same advice. Looking back now, I see that the advice was coming from a place of regret as they faced the end of their careers. I had no mentor at the time or anyone to guide me, so I listened to every word they said. They would all say some version of this: "I wish I would have bought a house when I was your age." This happened so many times I lost count. So I took the advice to heart and started buying houses at every opportunity. I was lucky enough to buy my first rental house at twenty while I still lived with my parents. Then I bought another house at twenty-two and moved into it. Shortly after that, I was lucky enough to read the book that had the biggest impact on my entire career: *Rich Dad Poor Dad* by Robert T Kiyosaki and Sharon Lechter. If you haven't read this book, then stop what you are doing and go buy it! The fundamentals of assets and the rat race are so simple and yet so profound. From that point on, real estate became my main source of creating income, but buying real estate assets became my career. The best analogy I can think of is building a snowman. An asset represents the ball you start with, and as you roll it in the snow, it gets larger. The longer you roll it, the bigger the snowball gets. So if you can get an asset early and let it roll for a long time, you will have a huge snowman at the end. The more time you have, the bigger the snowball. And if you want to supercharge the process, then you need more snow to create an army of snowmen.

The Basics

Have you ever heard of the flower called the white lotus? The slang term has a very interesting meaning. The white lotus is a beautiful flower that grows in swamps that are mucky and dirty, but it rises to the top and blooms pure white. From the outside, all you can see is a pretty flower, but if you look below the surface, it is dark, muddy, stinky, and not as it appears. Unfortunately, this is a good metaphor for many people's finances. On the outside, they look like they have it all together, they drive a nice car, live in a beautiful home, and go on fancy vacations. But when you look below the surface you will see they are in debt, missing payments, and living in a house of cards that is ready to come crashing down. Many realtors fall into this category, and it keeps them in bondage. Agents are famous for driving around in a BMW and going for lunches that extend into happy hour. Have you ever heard the saying, We buy things we don't need, with money we don't have, to impress people who don't care about us? We salespeople need to wake up and take control of our finances so we can start living life on our own terms and working towards financial freedom. A lot of salespeople don't want to be living the "white lotus" lifestyle; they simply haven't been taught the financial basics.

Basic #1: Spend less than you make! Another way to say this is that your revenue minus your expenses needs to be more than zero. This is the most basic step for financial literacy, but a lot of people don't seem to understand it. In real estate, this can become problematic because we live on inconsistent commissions. We need to have a higher financial literacy than an employee who makes an hourly wage.

First of all, we need to know the difference between wants and needs. Here is a basic table for you to use if you are starting from the beginning or need to work your way out of debt.

Needs	Wants
A place to live	A fancy house
Food	A fancy car
Transportation	College fund for your kids
Clothing	Eating out
Money to pay off debt	Vacations
	Fashion
	Entertainment

We can live on much less than we think we can. Until you have reached a certain level of financial security, you should live in a basic house, make your own food, and drive an economical vehicle to transport clients in. Anything beyond that will stand in the way of reaching your financial freedom in the future.

The very first step is paying off immediately any credit card debt, car loans, or payments on any other liabilities. The best way to do this is with a family budget. Budgets serve as a basic game plan to get you where you want to go. I cannot stress how important this step is. If you can't master living below your means on a budget, you will struggle in finances for the rest of your life, like so many people in the western world do.

Here is a goofy example from my life, but it is very appropriate to this topic of sticking to a budget. I love chips! They are my kryptonite. If there are chips in the house, I will find them, and I will eat them. Even on my most self-controlled days, I will break down just before bed and sneak a few salty bites. I soon learned that literally the only way I would not eat chips is if there were no chips in the house to be eaten. So if you have a credit card and you can't stop spending money on needless things, then cut up your card immediately. I know people who turn their paycheque into cash and put a certain amount of cash in different envelopes, one for groceries, one for gas, one for entertainment, etc. Then, when the envelope is empty, you're done spending in that area until your next paycheque.

Another piece of advice that will help you live within your means is to only buy vehicles with cash rather than with a loan or a lease. It is so easy to fall into the trap and rationalize your decision to finance a vehicle. Sneaky car salespeople will have you drowning in payments by convincing you to be proud of your new tax write-off. Since real estate is up and down, we need to do everything in our power to reduce consistent monthly payments, so only pay cash for a vehicle. Period.

As real estate agents, we are like small business owners, so our wants and needs chart needs to be a little more comprehensive. We must build in the basics to run a thriving business. An easy way to do this is to break down your commission cheques into percentages to help keep you on track. For example, say you get a $10,000 cheque. Thirty percent goes to tax, 20 percent goes to business expenses and future marketing, and the other 50 percent goes into your basic budget. How you run your basic budget is up to you. If you want to get ahead, I suggest allocating 20 percent of every cheque to a savings account for the purpose of buying assets. If you break this down, you are actually living off 30 percent of every commission cheque. When I share this with most agents, they turn pale because they are used to spending every dollar they make and living life with no plan. I promise that if you live on 30 percent now, you will thank me for it in the future. As time goes on, you will start to separate from the agents who spend every dollar they make. Over time, you will become wealthy and live life on your schedule with no financial stress while those other agents will still be chasing the next sale to keep up with their payments.

Basic #2. Change the way you view money. Money is NOT something we make for the purpose of spending. Money should be used to make more money. Since my twenties, I have pictured every dollar as a little money cartoon with arms and legs, and their job is to go find more money and bring it back to me. This means that money should be spent on assets that create more wealth in the long term. This is how your financial picture should look: take care of the basics with a budget, save money for assets, buy assets, and use cash flow from assets to live the life you want to live. It is so easy, but so few people actually do it.

Most people never reach financial freedom for two reasons. The first is lack of discipline and the lack of a plan. This causes people to live outside of their means and not make or stick to any sort of budget. The second reason is instant gratification. When impulses control our lives, we get caught up buying cars, spending on vacations and other things we don't need before we can afford them. Then you spend your whole life paying for things that are depreciating in value. We get caught running on a treadmill and never move forward. Trust me, I want you to go on that awesome vacation, drive an exotic Ferrari, and live in your dream home, but do not do it until you have enough assets to be able to afford it. In the next few chapters, I will dive into how to use assets to pay for your lifestyle so you don't have to sell houses to make a living.

Basic #3. Time is money. I bet you have heard this before. We need to understand this theory to be able to move towards financial freedom. Time is the most important asset we have, yet most of us spend our whole lives trading time for money. You have probably heard it said that our kids spell love T.I.M.E. Our kids don't care how much money we have, what they care about is how much time their dad and mom spend with them. If you get paid an hourly wage, you are literally getting paid for your time. If you want to make more money, you need to work more time. Unfortunately, too many of us get caught working long hours to pay for our expensive lifestyle and have no time to enjoy it. Instead, our goal should be to leverage things so we can make more money with less time. This is a simple principal, but few people understand it, so let's look at it in more detail.

Assets, Liabilities, and Leverage

This is where the fun begins. If you can get a handle on assets, liabilities, and leverage, you will set yourself up to live the life you want to live. This is where the rich get richer, and you can dream as big as you want. Before I dive into assets, I want to teach you about the difference between being financially wealthy and being rich. Our goal is to be wealthy, not rich, and I will explain why. If you are rich, it means you have a certain amount of money. Let's say you win the lottery and get five million dollars. The world would say you are rich in that moment. But it is common knowledge what happens to almost every lottery winner. That's right, they are all broke shortly afterwards, and they are left stunned and wondering where it all went. It is hard to believe, but people can blow five million dollars quickly. Here's how it looks. First you buy a Ferrari because you have always dreamed of owning one. Next, you buy a nice vacation home on the beach. You are feeling generous, so you pay off your parents' home and give some money to charity. Next, you take a trip around the world to see and taste the finer things in life. After a year, most of your money is gone, but your expenses are still high. The Ferrari is expensive to maintain, the lake house has high taxes and lots of maintenance, and you have no money coming in. Suddenly, you are aware that there is an end coming, and you can't stop it. Being rich has a time limit on it. Depending on your lifestyle, it might be one month, one year, or ten years, but the day will come when you run out of money. Being rich might be fun in the moment, but it won't last forever.

In contrast, wealth is not the amount of money you make, it is how long the money will last. Wealth has no time limit. For example, if you live on $2,000 per month and you have an asset that pays you $2,000 per month, you are truly wealthy because the well will never run dry. Wealth is what gives you your freedom. If you have more money coming in than you need (and no extra time is required) then you have done what most people only dream of. There is nothing better than working as a real estate agent because you want to and not because you have to. Clients will appreciate your advice because they know you are not in it for the commission but to truly add value to their lives.

So, what is an asset? An asset is anything that increases your income without spending your time. This can be a lot of different things and can range from stocks and bonds to businesses to car collections. An easy calculation is Asset + Time = More Money. For example, let's say you buy a stock at $100 per share and sell it a year later at $110 per share. You have just increased your money by ten dollars. I will not dive into stocks, car collections, or business, and I think most realtors shouldn't either. I am going to focus on real estate only because I think you should too. Ninety percent of all millionaires made their money through real estate and in one generation. Real estate is the simplest and safest asset you can own because over time, it only increases in value. They aren't making any more land, but we are increasing in population. That means that over time, more people are going to be competing for the same amount of land. Basic economics is supply and demand. If the supply of land cannot be increased, then the demand for it will. Property is also unique compared to the stock market. For example, in the stock market, you might invest in a great company in a good industry, but if the world thinks it isn't green or an accountant cooked the books, the company can go broke, and you will lose everything. Real estate is very risk-free if you have a long-term perspective. As a real estate agent, you are a professional in the industry, so you should have a head start in buying great real estate assets. In my opinion, this is the secret weapon of our industry. We will have access to the best deals and will have the best insight into the market, which is a recipe for success. If every agent focused on buying a couple of rental properties throughout their career, then they would retire a lot wealthier.

It's also important to define an asset in real estate a little bit further. An asset puts money in your pocket, it does not take it out. This means that your personal house does not count. Yes, it's an asset that gains value over time, but it also costs you money to hold it. You have to pay insurance, tax, utilities, interest on a mortgage, etc. Many people live outside of their means and buy a big, fancy house while rationalizing that it is an asset. They work all year just to pay the bills for their house. Some houses can cost people over $50,000 per year if they were to actually do the math. You have to pay to live somewhere, so I do recommend buying your personal house, but do not consider it an asset on your way to financial freedom.

Leverage is rarely talked about and is another secret weapon in the real estate asset business. The simplest definition for leverage is to use something that you already have in order to achieve something new or better. Leverage is also the reason why real estate will always outperform the stock market. Financial advisers can be sneaky when trying to get you to invest. They will say that the stock market returns 8 percent annually on average, while the real estate market only averages 6 percent. Then they go on to say that real estate still needs maintenance, insurance, and other costs to keep it running. They are not wrong, but they purposely remove leverage from the conversation so they can compete for your money. Once you introduce leverage, they are no longer in the same sandbox as us. If you can use the bank's money, then you can leverage your own money. This has been the single biggest reason why I have been able to financially get ahead in life. I will show you an example.

Stock market: You take $100,000 and put it in a stock for twenty-five years that averages 8 percent returns. After twenty-five years you will have **$684,847.52**. That is pretty good!

Real estate: You take $100,000 and use it for a down payment on a rental property. The bank required 20 percent down, so you buy a house for $500,000 with your $100,000 down payment. The interest rate is 4 percent. The rent received is $2,600 per month and your mortgage payment is $2,111 per month. Including all your costs, the total monthly expenses for this property is $2,350. Therefore, you cash flow $150 per month. Let's see where this ends up after twenty-five years. The house will be worth $2,145,935.36 after twenty-five years, and the mortgage will be fully paid off. Further, the cash flow of $150 per month over twenty-five years will have added up to $90,000. The total after twenty-five years would be **$2,235,935.**

As you can see, the power of leverage allows you to make an extra $1,551,088 after twenty-five years. This is why every piece of real estate you own should always be leveraged. The old idea of paying off your property will only hurt you financially. You are better off increasing your mortgage to go buy a second property with the extra money. This is exactly how I built my real estate portfolio to what it is today. When I bought my first rental property, I cashed flowed about $1,000 per month. This extra money was used to pay for my vehicle, gas, and insurance. I later refinanced that property and bought another house and had two houses paying me $1,000 per month each. Now, my groceries, gas, and insurance were being paid while these two assets were increasing in value and paying down the mortgage. I have continued using this principle of leverage and will continue implementing it in the future. If you do it correctly, you can double your real estate portfolio every five years without the addition of money from an outside source. This is why I am able to have roughly thirty rental doors before the age of forty. Once the snowball starts rolling, it is fun to watch it grow.

Know your Assets

We need to realize what makes a good real estate asset and why. Most people can't describe what a good real estate asset is, which is why realtors get stuck doing false advertising on their properties. When they have a terrible house that is full of issues and in a bad location, they will promote it by saying "investor alert." When I ask them why it's a good investment, they say things like, "well, when you fix it up, it will be worth more money," or "a little sweat equity and you will have a great property." These answers show that they have very little understanding of what a good real estate investment it.

Let's get into the basics of understanding what a good asset is and why we buy them. It is very important to know why we are investing in a certain property and what the exit strategy is. A good recommendation is to have a little investment book and take notes on why you are making a purchase. Every rental property has three benefits: principal repayment, appreciation, and cash flow. Which one of those three is most important to you? This will be different for every investor depending on what stage they are in. For example, a new investor might require cash flow because they are tight on money. If you look at the investment property over twenty-five years, the only one of the three benefits that is guaranteed is principal repayment. If interest rates rise, then the cash flow will diminish or disappear, or if there is a short-term declining market, then the property will not appreciate for that period of time. But principal repayment will always be present, so I always teach investors that you need to be okay with the steady and slow process of paying down a mortgage if you are going to be an investor.

I like to use the analogy of going for dinner to help explain your investment strategy. Every dinner has the option of an appetizer, a main course, and a dessert. When I go for dinner with my wife, we go because of the main course. Think of principal paydown as the main course. Once in a while, if we have extra time, we will get an appetizer before dinner. This always makes the dinner seem more fun. The appetizer is like cash flow on an investment: it isn't always there, but when rents go up and interest rates on mortgages go down, then we will get cash flow for a while. And finally, there is dessert (this is definitely my wife's favourite part). We don't always get dessert, but we sure enjoy it when we do. Appreciation on real estate is like the dessert: properties won't always go up in value, but when they do, it sure is fun.

Pro Formas

Pro formas are simply a cash projection into the future that shows how much a property or business investment will make over a certain period of time. Usually it is three to five years, but it can be even longer. These are amazing tools for analyzing investments since they keep our decisions based on numbers and not on emotions. Even though pro formas are not taught in any real estate course, every realtor must know how to create and use them if they want to take their business to the next level. Pro formas must be used for investors, developers, and even regular buyers. They provide a window into the future, and are much simpler than you think. The pro forma summarizes revenue, expenses, cash flow, return on investment (ROI), and return on invested capital (ROIC). For me, it has always been a great first step in analyzing any investment. Typically, I will not consider a property unless I get an ROIC of 15 percent or more. Every investor will have their own threshold depending on several factors. A newer investor might be willing to take more risks because they have time on their side and are willing to chase a higher ROIC, while a mature investor with less time might search for a lower ROIC that is safer. It all depends on what your goals are. For example, you might buy a property in a bad location because you know future development is on the way. You will have to deal with bad tenants and a rundown house, but in the future it will really pay off.

If you provide pro forma to your investor-clients, you will separate yourself from most realtors. This is a great service and will guarantee you referrals and clients for life. Think about it: many realtors will call a client and say, "Investor alert! You should buy this property; I think it's a good deal." Clients will be skeptical because why would they blindly take the advice of the realtor who just wants to make a commission? What if instead of this "investor alert," you send them a property along with pro forma and conclude with: "This looks like a great investment. The ROI is 15 percent per year and the area is really gaining future value." This will build confidence with your client, and I promise they will tell their friends and family about the value that you bring to them. It is also important to know that veteran investors will require this, so if you want work with sophisticated real estate clients, you better know how to do this in your sleep.

Building Pro Forma

I don't want to go into too much detail on this subject, but it will require some expertise. Every market is different and will have different inputs. Each pro forma will require five basic principles:

1. **The total cost to acquire an asset.** This includes down payment, any taxes, fees from professionals, renovations

required, etc. You must make sure these inputs are correct and add them into your spreadsheet.

2. **Revenue produced by the asset.** This is pretty straightforward but is often done incorrectly by salespeople who will overestimate the rent received in order to make the numbers seem better. Do not do this. I highly recommend a few things to get your revenue correct. First, you should take the average of the last five years of monthly rent amounts in order to get a more conservative number. Next, you should get a couple of local property managers to give you their estimation of the rent. This way, you will never over-promise and under-deliver to your client. There is nothing worse than telling a client they will get a certain return on investment, and they find out later it was not possible.

3. **Total monthly expenses.** We must gather up all the expenses incurred to own the property on a yearly basis. This includes but is not limited to taxes, insurance, vacancy rates, repairs and maintenance, utilities, management fees, and mortgage payments. Again, check everything to make sure the numbers are accurate and nothing is missed. Things like vacancy rates and taxes can be easily found, while repairs and maintenance will depend on the type of property purchased.

4. **Put all the variables into a spreadsheet.** This is where we do our net calculations. It is simply the gross revenue minus the total expenses to get our net profit. This is just a basic income statement for those of us who didn't go to business school.

5. **Future Forecast.** Once we have our net profit or loss, we can begin an accurate forecast of the future. This can be a difficult process to explain, but there is a great visual example that can be found in the Content Lounge of elevatecoachingco.com. If we are doing a five-year pro forma estimation, then these are the calculations I want to consider: principal repayment over five years, cash flow estimation over five

years, and finally, the appreciation of the asset over five years. I like to break the appreciation into a few calculations so I can give a conservative outlook if the market doesn't do anything in five years, and I like to do an average calculation if the market performs at an average rate. It looks like this:

$500,000 property if the market rises 1% per year for 5 years. Future value is $525,505

$500,000 property if the market rises 4% per year. Future value is $608,326

$500,000 property if the market rises 7% per year. Future value is $701,275

Most markets average 7 percent per year, but I like to give conservative calculations to clients, so they aren't disappointed if the returns don't work out how they wanted. As you can see, it's pretty easy to make $201,275 in appreciation over five years in an average market, and that doesn't even factor in principal repayment or cash flow.

The ability to put together pro formas will revolutionize your ability to work with investors and help your personal portfolio as well. If you go to elevatecoachingco.com you will have the opportunity to get access to a template through the contact lounge.

Acquiring your First Asset

I want realtors to be wildly successful and live a life of adventure and wealth. In order to do this, you must buy and hold real estate assets throughout your career. Just selling houses will not be good enough. Even if you are a top producing agent, the chances of retiring wealthy are very low because most people live very close to their income and therefore never build up a nest egg. I have worked with doctors who make huge money but have to work late into life because they did not invest and instead lived a lavish lifestyle. Realtors are the same in my experience. I want to save us from ourselves! If we can get that first real estate asset, we increase our chances of living a successful life of adventure and wealth. If we can get just one, everything will be different. There are many laws in our life that we live with every day, like the fact that we can't escape gravity, and that light always overtakes darkness. Another one that speaks directly to acquiring your first asset is that the first one is always the hardest. After you acquire one, it becomes easier and easier to grow your portfolio because it starts to grow on its own.

I know several agents who work seven days a week from dawn till dusk, who will never make as much money as an average agent who owns several assets. So if you want to be a salesperson that retires wealthy, your next step is to buy your first real estate asset (remember your personal house does not count). It is easier than you think, and I want to give you a few strategies to help get you there. This might sound weird, but first you need to have the desire and the end goal in mind. If you have a goal that you care about, there is no reason you will not achieve it.

When I was twenty-one, I remember being at a party with some friends, and after a few drinks I proclaimed that I wanted to be worth $1 million at thirty, $10 million at forty, and $100 million by fifty. I almost felt embarrassed to say it out loud, but in my heart, I knew it was possible. That was the goal I needed, I had the desire to do it, and now that I had said it out loud, I wouldn't let myself fail. What is your goal? What are your desires in life? At the time, my favourite magazine was called *National Geographic Adventure*, and its slogan was: *dream it, plan it, do it.* That stuck with me and when I said my dream out loud when I was twenty-one, I began turning it into a plan. I love teaching people how to buy their first asset because it turns their dreams into a plan.

Now that we have a dream, let's start the plan. In general, a bank will require 20 percent down on an investment property. The down payment is the number one thing that stops a person from buying their first asset. So how do we get that down payment? There are many, many ways to do this. Let's do some math.

If we want to buy a $500,000 property, we need to have $100,000. That seems like a lot of money, but for realtors this is easier than we think. If the average commission per transaction is 3 percent then a $500,000 sale pays $15,000 dollars. That means we need seven transactions to save an extra $105,000. If we write our own offer, then we only need six extra sales. This is achievable for any agent. If you follow the steps laid out in this book, six extra sales will not be difficult.

Once I was building a commercial building that was 12,000 sq. ft. It had five apartments above and 6,000 sq. ft. of office space below that I was planning to use for my new office. The bank told me I needed 20 percent down, which at the time was about $500,000 dollars. Further, they said that they wanted me to put my equity in first, and they would do draws later based off the progress of construction. Then came a day I will never forget. The bank manager called me into his office to have a meeting. I thought: How nice! He wants to say congratulations on building such a nice property and maybe talk about the final mortgage when everything was complete. I could not have been more wrong. I entered his office, and immediately I could tell something was off. He sat me down and went into this long monologue about the real estate market and how he thought we were in a bubble. He didn't seem to have any point, so after five minutes, I interrupted and asked him why I was in his office. He proceeded to say, sorry, we have lost our appetite to finance this project. You are going to have to hit the road and find a new bank. I was shocked. My hands started to sweat, and I could feel my stomach start churning. I was down to my last dollar and construction was in full swing. How was I going to pay the trades, let alone finish the building? I live in a small city and reputation is everything. Not only did I have a chance of going broke, I also was going to lose my reputation. So I did what the banker told me to do, and I hit the road immediately looking for a new bank. It's funny how motivating the fear of failure can be! Within the week, I had already met with several bankers, and two of them said that they were happy to finish the project for me. The only catch was that they needed 35 percent down instead of 20 percent. I had no one in my life at that time who would lend me the money, so I did the only thing I knew how to do. I sold as many houses as possible and saved up the commission money. At the time, the average commission was $6,700, so I needed to sell thirty more houses. It required seven days a week of open houses and working all hours, but I did it. I sold thirty more properties and came up with the money. I believe that any realtor can sell more houses if they want to come up with a down payment to buy a rental property.

Another way to get the down payment is to sell things you don't need. Remember the plan. First you buy assets, *then* you buy the other things that you don't need. If you have a boat, RV, fancy car, etc., sell those things to get a down payment for your first asset. Give up the immediate for the long term, and I promise you will be glad you did. We can all live far simpler than we think we can. Evaluate your life, and drop everything that isn't necessary until you have saved for that down payment for your first asset.

Refinancing assets to buy more assets is another great way to grow your portfolio. For example, let's say you have owned your own house for ten years, but you haven't bought an asset yet. Most likely, you have a ton of equity in your home. For example, if you paid $300,000 for your house ten years ago, then it's probably worth $600,000 today and the mortgage balance is probably below $250,000. That means that you have roughly $350,000 of equity in the house. A bank will require that you have at least 5 percent down in your home, but let's be conservative and keep 10 percent of the equity in the home. That means we can refinance the mortgage to $540,000 and take the rest of the money as cash. This means that you will be able to take out $290,000 cash for your next down payment (New mortgage: $540,000 – existing mortgage: $250,000 = $290,000). If you have $290,000 and you need 20 percent down this means you can buy an asset up to $1,450,000.

The last way to get a down payment is to borrow it from another source. This should be a last resort but should not be overlooked as it can be very beneficial. Borrowing money helps speed up the process of growing your assets. It gives you a head start on the "time value" of your money. Understanding the "time value" of money is an important concept. What it means is that your money should increase over time if invested properly. Consider this question: would you rather have received $1 million dollars ten years ago or $1.5 million today? The answer is $1 million ten years ago because if you invested that money back then and got a return of 7 percent a year, it would be worth $1,967,151 now. We want to get our money working for us a soon as possible even if borrowing the down payment is necessary to make it happen.

Let's review the process of borrowing for a down payment. If you are going to ask someone for money, make sure you have a plan. Don't just ask someone you know for $100,000 and say you will pay them back in a few years. Especially as a real estate agent, this looks so unprofessional. Instead, write a plan to the investor about how you will both benefit from the transaction. There are many ways to structure a deal, but some easy examples are offering them higher interest rates, a percent of ownership, or a balloon payment at the end. Whatever way you decide, make sure you have a clear written agreement between the two of you. The written agreement should be looked over by an attorney and agreed upon by all parties.

A few years ago, there was another commercial property I really wanted, but I didn't have the down payment. I needed a million dollars, and I wasn't able to save it or refinance any of my other properties in time for me to make an offer. The property was an amazing deal, and I did not want to miss it. I needed to borrow the money from someone, so I went to one of the mentors in my life. This woman has been instrumental in my career, so I brought her a plan. I was willing to pay an interest rate that was 4.5 percent above the bank rate, and I needed it for one year. Additionally, I signed an agreement allowing her to put a second mortgage on a different property I owned in case something went wrong, and it didn't work. She gave me the $1 million dollars I needed, and I bought the property for $3.6 million dollars. I did some improvements and rented the whole building out. In less than a year, I refinanced and pulled out the $1 million dollars to pay her back. This ended up being a win-win situation. She made good interest on her money, and I was able to buy an undervalued building in an amazing location. That was five years ago. Since then, I have made plans to knock the building over and put up 89 apartments and 20,000 sq. ft. of commercial space. The property is now worth about $9 million dollars and I have paid off over $300,000 in principal since I bought it. In five years, I will have made over $5 million dollars on the property if I wanted to sell it. That is a pretty good profit in five years when I didn't even have the down payment. This is an example of how borrowing money can really increase the time value of your money.

Know Your Assets

We are real estate professionals and should know what makes a good real estate investment. We have learned that principal repayment is the most important factor followed by cash flow and appreciation, but we need to be pros on how to select the best asset. A good investment is not always the cheapest. The fixer-uppers and investment alerts are usually the ones you should steer clear of. When I evaluate an asset, I focus on three things: tenant profile, condition of the property, and the location. All three of these matter and should be considered when purchasing a property.

Tenant Profile

This means I focus on the type of person who will be renting the asset. You want a person who takes care of the property and always pays rent. You have worked hard for your money, and you deserve to have a good experience purchasing a piece of real estate. If you look for the cheapest house in a bad area, I promise that you will have a bad experience. The type of tenant that rents your property will have a big impact on your future returns, and you need to consider this. A house in good condition and in a good location will usually attract a better tenant. I am generalizing, and, of course, there are exceptions to this rule, but you must consider the type of person who will rent your property. If it is near an elementary school, you are likely to get a young family. If it is an apartment near a university, you are likely to get a student. If the house is in bad condition and in a rough part of town, then you might attract a type of tenant that you will not have a good experience with. Always, always consider the type of tenant you want before you purchase an investment property.

I bought my first rental when I was twenty years old. The world had not been cruel to me, and I believed the best in people. I bought a half-duplex that was new and near a school. On paper,

I had bought a great property and should have attracted a great tenant, but I got a bad apple, and it was all my fault. Hopefully you can learn from my mistakes. Mistake number one was that I rented to the first person who applied. I did not do any kind of background check like calling her past landlords. She told me she was from a local church, had a nice dog, was on government assistance, and needed to rent right away. I thought, great! She can move in right away, and she must be a good person if she goes to church. Red flag number 1: If someone can move in right away, that means they have not given proper notice to their last landlord and are leaving them high and dry. Red flag number 2: Just because someone goes to church does not mean they are a great person. Red flag number 3: Pets, for the most part, do not belong in homes, and they will wreck your house faster than you can imagine. So she moved in, and everything was awesome. The mortgage was $1,100 per month and she was paying $1,300. I was paying down a mortgage and collecting $200 per month while I was living with my parents rent-free.

Everything was good until the six-month mark. At the start of the month, she said she would be a little late on rent because something bad had happened and asked if I could be patient. I said, no problem and collected the rent ten days late. I covered the mortgage myself but still got rent that month, so everything was still okay. Then the next month came, and I got the same call, except this time she said she couldn't pay till the end of the month. Again, I said no problem, since she was in a rough spot. The rent came on the 20th, but I made it work again out of my own pocket. When the same thing happened the next month, I knew she was taking advantage of me. She called and said she would be late, but this time would pay me a late bonus since she couldn't get her money till the end of the month. The end of the month came, and she paid her rent, but now couldn't pay the next month's rent. Things were starting to spiral. I thought it was time to pay her a visit and tell her that she needed to catch up on the rent. So I met her at the house, but the weirdest thing happened: she didn't let me in. Instead, she stepped out onto the front step to talk to me, closing the door behind her so I couldn't see into the house. She said she was in a rough place and asked me to be patient with her. Christmas was coming, and she needed some extra time to catch up on her late rent. I reluctantly said yes because I felt sorry for her and believed the story she was telling me. Now I was two months behind on rent with no plan on getting it back. Then December 1st came, and she was now three months behind. I decided I would pay her a visit without calling first because I didn't trust her anymore and I sincerely needed the rent. It was just above freezing and pouring rain when I arrived. To my surprise, every door and window was wide open, and the house was trashed. The windows and doors had been open for days, and she had not turned off her utility accounts so I would get those bills as well. I stepped into the living room, and in the middle of the floor was a pile of feces as a final parting gift from her to me. I never heard from her again and I was left to pick up the pieces.

I hope you can learn from my mistakes. Since then, I have had hundreds of tenants and for the most part, they have been great. I always call a potential tenant's previous two landlords and their employer. Also, I don't allow pets. I check out their social media accounts to see what type of people they are. I have found that when people say they don't drink or do drugs, then they probably do. I would never think of telling a landlord that I don't do drugs or drink because that isn't part of my lifestyle. I also always ask to sign the tenant agreement at their current house as a way to check if it is in good condition. If they don't want to meet there, I assume they are someone who won't take care of the property.

Condition of the Property

The next consideration when purchasing an asset is the condition of the property. As a rule of thumb, I want properties that are seven years old or newer because there will be a low chance of major expenses, and they will attract better tenants. As properties get older, more things wear out and break down. Roofs leak, foundations crack, furnaces break down, and these can all cost a lot of money to fix, which will take away from the performance of an asset. Most properties aren't built to last more than twenty-five years without upgrades, so if you buy something newer and sell it before these items come up, then you will maximize your returns. Another option is an older property that has been completely renovated to like-new condition.

Location

A good location will usually cost more, but you will also net higher returns and have better tenants. As a professional in your area, you will know where the good locations are. I advise against buying a cheaper property in a bad location for several reasons. When the market is bad, it will become nearly impossible to sell, whereas properties in good locations are sellable in any market. You want to target an asset that 80 percent of buyers would want to own. Poor locations also don't appreciate as much as good locations. People with high paying jobs want to be in the good locations, therefore assets will do better in these locations. Just like we target good tenants now, we also want to target a good buyer for when we sell our asset in the future.

It can also be wise to invest in an area that is currently a bad location, but you know it will get better. This isn't for the faint of heart, but it can bring great results. This reemphasizes the importance of being aware of your city and what development plans it has in the future. For example, if an area is upzoned to higher density, it might be a good idea to buy a property in that area and hold it until an apartment is approved for it. If you are buying in a bad location for the potential of improvement, then make sure you have the long game in mind because sometimes it can take longer than you think. I know some people who have bought properties that will pass down to their kids because they know it will take fifty years for the city to grow in that area.

How to Retire: Beginning with the End in Mind

So why did I spend so much time talking about investing in a book that is a guide for real estate salespeople? I did it because I believe investing is the whole point. Real estate sales is an amazing career, and we have access to the best properties and the best deals for the duration of our careers, and we need to take advantage of this. Sales is a lot of fun and can be very rewarding, but few realtors retire wealthy, and I want to change this. Too many realtors give everything to their career and to their clients and it costs them their financial freedom. I want you to retire wealthy and have the freedom you desire.

So here is a guide to retiring wealthy, and I believe that every single salesperson has the ability to do it. Earlier in the book, I talked about treating the first five years like a university degree by learning everything you can and mastering the skills you need to become a mature realtor. After five years, your income will explode, and it will be time to shift your focus to acquiring assets for your retirement. If you do it right, you should be making at least $150,000 per year and most people will be making a lot more than that. It's important after year five to not increase your spending. It's so tempting to buy that new car or boat or bigger house with the extra income, but this still isn't the time. Years six to ten should be all about acquiring assets.

We know that the path is in the math, so let's look at what a plan to retire wealthy looks like:

You are thirty years old and start your real estate journey, and the goal is to retire wealthy at age fifty. (Thirty is just an example. It can be forty or even fifty. It's never too late!)

Years 1 to 5 are spent learning and building a great database of clients who will use you for life. At the end of year 5, you are confident in the business you have built and have great systems in place to ensure you will have consistent income for years to come.

Year 6 (you are thirty-six now) and your income is $150,000 after taxes. You are able to live off $80,000 and the other $70,000 is left to invest. So let's buy a property that is worth $375,000. As a rule of thumb, the rent should be roughly 1 percent of the total purchase price, but let's do .75 percent to be extra conservative. So the rent received per month is $2,812. The mortgage will be $300,000 and the monthly mortgage payment at 4 percent will be $1,578. That gives you $1,234 to use to pay taxes, insurance, and any other expenses. After expenses, you should have at least $300 per month in net cash flow.

Year 7 and your income is $180,000 after taxes. You are still able to live off $80,000 and the other $100,000 you are able to invest. So you buy a second rental property at $500,000 with your 20 percent down payment of $100,000. The rent received is $3,750 and the mortgage is $2,104 per month. That gives you $1,646 left to pay for the other expenses. After you have paid these, your net cash flow is $500 per month.

Year 8 and your income is $200,000 after taxes. You are able to live off of $80,000 and the other $120,000 is left to invest. So you buy a property that is worth $600,000. The rent received per month is $4,500. The mortgage will be $480,000 and the monthly mortgage payment at 4 percent will be $2,524. That gives you $1,976 to pay for taxes, insurance, and any other expenses. After expenses, you should have at least $700 per month in net cash flow.

Year 9 and your income is $220,000 after taxes. You are able to live off of $80,000 and the other $140,000 is left to invest. So let's buy a property that is worth $700,000. The rent received per month is $5,250. The mortgage will be $560,000 and the monthly mortgage payment at 4 percent will be $2,945. That gives you $2,305 to pay for taxes, insurance, and any other expenses. After expenses, you should have at least $900 per month in net cash flow.

Year 10 and your income is $250,000 after taxes. You have just turned forty, and you now have four rental properties and have been grinding for ten years. It's time to live a little, so you decide to enjoy this year a little more. You pay cash for that $100,000 car you have always wanted, and you go on a few vacations. You spend $200,000 of your money and put the other $50,000 in a savings account for the future.

I understand that numbers can get boring, but stay with me. The path is always in the math.

Year 20. You are now fifty years old, and you want to retire wealthy. Let's take a look at your finances. I am assuming you have kept the properties and have not refinanced or done anything major. Let's also assume you were able to save $20,000 per year from year 10 to 20 since you didn't buy any other assets and you now have a nest egg of $200,000 cash. The market has risen at 7 percent per year and mortgage rates have stayed at 4 percent on all your mortgages to make the math easy.

- Property 1: Value is $966,950, the mortgage remaining is $210,227, your equity is $756,723.
- Property 2: Value is $1,204,922, the mortgage remaining is 300,951, your equity is $903,971.
- Property 3: Value is $1,351,314, the mortgage remaining is $384189, your equity is $967,125.
- Property 4: Value is $1,473,396, the mortgage remaining is $474,067, your equity is $999,329.

The total equity you have at this point is over $3.6 million dollars, and I haven't even factored in the cash flow on any of the properties. At this point, you have so many options. Remember that was our goal—to retire wealthy and live a life of freedom. You can keep holding the properties and refinance one property every year to take out a lump sum tax-free. You can sell all the properties and put the money in the bank. You can keep the properties, and they will soon be paid off, and by sixty, your monthly income will be over $16,312 per month from the four properties.

Can you see how unbelievable this is? Every realtor can retire wealthy. If every agent was taught this from the beginning and followed this guide, we would all live the lives we desired. We forget how many opportunities there are when we learn how to make our money work for us, including becoming a better realtor than the competition because of the expertise gained through your own experience of acquiring assets.

Chapter 11: Goals: Dream it, Plan it, Do it

I would argue most people have a negative view on goals. Too many of us have set a goal and not reached it. If you do this enough times, you will lose confidence in yourself and hesitate to set yourself up for another failure. Sometimes it is easier to not set a goal so you don't have another personal failure. The trouble with this attitude is you will not become the person you want to be. Time will pass and you will still be the same person, year after year after year. Setting goals is an incredibly personal thing and should be something you do for yourself and not for other people. In my early twenties I found this magazine called National Geographic Adventure Magazine. On the cover of every edition was the simple text that said: dream it, plan it, do it. When I read this it ignited something in my soul. It seemed so simple. All I had to do was dream it, then plan it, and then do it. It was the easiest formula of all time. I would flip through the pages and picture myself going on these amazing adventures around the world. Then something so simple and so incredible happened. It was a shift in the person I was. I gave myself permission to move out of the dreaming stage into a state of action. I always wanted to experience new adventures, but I never really knew what to do next. It makes me laugh thinking about it today because it seems so elementary. However, if you look at most people in our world they dream of all sorts of things, but none of them take action. I don't want you to be just a dreamer! I want you to be a dreamer, then planner, then doer.

As a kid, I read a book in elementary school called *Banner in the Sky*. It was the first book about adventure I had read, and I pictured myself climbing big mountains when I grew up. As I was reading the *National Geographic Adventure Magazine*, I suddenly imagined myself climbing Mt. Everest. In that moment, I knew my next step was to plan it, then do it. The next day I called one of my friends and said let's go to Mt. Everest. He said yes at first, so I began planning. As time went on reality hit, and he decided to back out. This is so typical of goal setting. We have an idea and start to do it, but quickly back out when the rubber hits the road. So I had a choice to make. Was I going to be just a dreamer, or would I take action on my dreams? A life filled with dreams and no action seems like a life of regret to me, so I took one of my first major leaps. I decided to go on a solo trip, where I met up with a group of unknown hikers for three weeks in the Himalayas of Nepal and hiked to Mt. Everest base camp. It was the adventure of a lifetime and one of my fondest memories in life. I met so many amazing people and experienced some of the coolest moments in my life. This adventure was made possible because of a magazine that said, *dream it, plan it, do it*. Never forget this simple formula! Sometimes the most profound things are the simplest. This formula has allowed me to realize so many of my dreams. If I can dream it, then I can do it and so can you. Never forget that.

The first step to elevating your life is setting goals that are defined by what you want to achieve. You must have a clear idea of exactly what it is you want to accomplish. Spend some time dreaming, or surround yourself with other dreamers if you are having trouble. Ask yourself what it is that you actually want. Some goals you might set are selling fifty homes, running a marathon, starting a business, canoeing the Amazon, or hiring an assistant. Setting a clear goal is simple, but it can fall off the rails quickly if you don't do it right. Most people set goals and see what happens rather than building a plan around those goals. The first thing you need to do is have a rough vision of what you want your life to look like at certain times in the future. This can be five years, or ten years, or even more. This vision must include all the different facets of your life such as career, personal growth, health, friends and family, romance, spirituality, finance, and recreation. We get one shot at this life, so it's important to think about the life you want to live. My core values centre around adventure, family, influence, freedom, helping others, and living an active lifestyle, therefore my goals reflect this.

I really want to hammer down on this point because it isn't what most of us are taught. We are usually taught to only set goals for things like weight loss or our career. Currently 59 percent of young adults eighteen to thirty-four set New Year's resolutions. In the first week, 23 percent of people quit, by day thirty, another 36 percent of people stop, and after one year, only 9 percent of young adults managed to complete their resolution. Those are really bad odds, and I want to change them for you. I want you to be able to dream it, plan it, and do it in any area of life that you desire. A major reason that goals and resolutions fail is because the goal was set to please other people. I want your goals to come from your gut. I want you to know deep inside yourself that each goal you set is truly what you want. You must set your goals around your dreams.

One way to set goals that accurately reflect what your dreams are is to take a personal retreat all alone with no devices: just you and a notepad. Another way is to find a good course, coach, or mentor to learn from and set you on the right path. However you go about deciding what your dreams and goals are, never forget to consider the person you will be if you achieve those goals. Remember when you say yes to something you are also saying no to something else. For example, if you set a goal to sell two hundred homes a year, think about who you will become in the process and what you will have to say no to. Will you have the time to build a relationship with your kids, take care of your health, or go on any adventures? I can't answer that question for you, but when you go about setting goals for your future, remember to include all the different facets of your life: career, personal growth, health, friends and family, romance, spirituality, finance, and recreation.

I learned this lesson the hard way when I first started setting goals. I remember setting a goal early in my career to sell sixty homes per year, which came down to five sales a month. I wrote it down in my office so I could see it every day. If the month was coming to an end, and I didn't have five sales, I would go hunting for deals and find a buyer so that I wouldn't miss the mark. I made my targets every month and hit the goal of sixty homes that year, so the next year I made it seventy-five homes. When I hit that target, I made it one hundred. I was so excited to hit those big numbers that I failed to realize who I was becoming or why I was even setting those goals in the first place. If I had been completely honest with myself, I was working seven days a week trying to prove I wasn't a failure. Even though I was selling a lot of homes, I wasn't becoming the person I wanted to be. I was overweight, not sleeping, missing out on adventures, and had little time for my friends or family. I was also giving up lots of my other dreams. Many people around me paid the price, including my spouse. My goal for you is to be much more successful in goal planning than I was. I want you to stay on track and be proud of the person you are becoming.

Today, I have a basic vision of who I want to be and of the core values that motivate me. I set goals for more than just selling houses. At the beginning of every year, I do a full evaluation of all my previous goals and build a new plan to stay in line with the person I want to become. Currently, I set relationship goals for my wife and kids, I set goals for adventure, I set goals for health, I set goals for my business, and for the person I want to become. When you set goals in all of these areas, your chance of success will be much higher, and your soul will feel a lot more satisfied. Everything in our life is connected, so it doesn't make sense to set goals for business and no other area of our lives.

Create a loose vision for your life that includes all the areas you want to improve in. From there, write down the individual goal for each category and break it down using the SMART goal setting theory, making sure each goal is S- Specific, M-Measurable, A- Achievable, R-Relevant, and T-Time bound. Everyone knows what SMART goals are. Here is how it might look:

Goal number one: To make $600,000 dollars per year.

> Specific: Sell sixty homes per year since the average commission is $10,000.

> Measurable: Five sales per month.

> Achievable: Five open houses per week. Database of one hundred clients to hear from me once per month for twelve months. Hunt great deals every month as needed.

Relevant: This gets me to the goal of making $600k so I can live a life of adventure and giving back.

Time bound: One year to complete the goal.

Goal number 2: To be a great father.

Specific: Love is spelled T-I-M-E for kids. Spend daily time with my kids (without my phone) plus two trips per year to build memories.

Measurable: Two hours per day of intentional time plus booking two short trips. One trip will be in July for an overnight hiking trip, the other trip will be three days in Disneyland.

Achievable: Be home by 5:00 p.m. every day and spend two hours of intentional time with the kids five days per week. Book both trips by January 30.

Relevant: I want my kids to feel loved unconditionally and supported by me. I also want to prepare my kids to be successful and functional adults. Spending time with them and being intentional about a relationship is how I will accomplish this.

Time bound: This is a one-year goal and will be tweaked every year to help improve our relationship.

These are just a couple of examples, but hopefully it paints a picture of the importance of setting goals for more than just selling houses. Selling houses becomes more achievable when your goal is to become financially free instead of selling lots of homes so that you can get lots of awards. I have taught many of my realtors this principal. A goal that has a vision behind it becomes much more powerful and achievable. Hopefully now you have the tools to dream it, plan it, and do it.

Micro-commitments and habits.

Goals can be intimidating, while small commitments are easily achieved. Throughout our lives, we set goals that are not always achieved, and that can lead to setting fewer goals because we feel like we won't meet them anyway. We are human and daily self-control can be difficult. You might set a goal of calling five people on your database per day for a year, but after one month, you run out of steam and find excuses not to do it. Then, because you are failing at your goal, you give it up altogether. I don't want this to happen in your life and in your career, so I want to shift you into a posture of success.

Big goals are great, but a habit is how you meet those goals. When you focus on habits and micro-commitments, you will elevate your life and career. If you eat clean and work out every day, I bet you will have a six pack. If you run every day, then running a marathon in two years will be easy. If you call people on your database every day, you will sell a lot of homes. If you do open houses every week, you will pick up buyers. Do you see how this works? Instead of focusing on the huge goals, focus on the habits that will get you to those goals. If you can create a habit and stick to it every day, you will meet your goals, even the big ones. It's my personal mantra to MEDC (Make Every Day Count). If you make every day count on a consistent basis, you will be unstoppable in anything you put your mind to.

Let's apply habits and micro-commitments to our careers in sales to see how this principle works. We need to first have a morning habit. Many gurus will tell you to get up at 5:00 a.m., go to the gym, meditate, stretch, eat a clean breakfast, wake the family up and be working by 9:00 a.m. If I got up at 5:00 a.m. every day, I would burn out and be useless in the evening when I'm with my family. I have met very few people who are able to get up at 5:00 a.m. and follow that kind of a routine before work every day. A successful habit must be something that is achievable for you. For me, an achievable time to wake up is any time after 6:30am. My body also hates exercise first thing in the morning—it is just how I was made! Our bodies are all different, and the rhythm of how we function varies from person to person. When and how we eat, exercise, learn, and work efficiently is unique to each of us. What is important is to listen to your body and build your habits based on the rhythm of your specific body. Your body will thank you, and habits will become a part of who you are. It took me years to get this right, but my morning habits are now built around the best flow for my body. I already laid out my morning routine earlier in the book, but I want to reemphasize the importance of a morning routine every single day to help you reach your goals. I spend an hour and twenty minutes before 9:00 a.m. reviewing what I might have missed from the day before and planning out my day. Your morning habits need to be simple and consistent, and you need a minimum of thirty minutes of planning before your day starts. This can also happen the night before. I know many successful realtors who think best at night and are terrible in the morning, so before they go to bed, they write a list of everything they need to do the next day in order to achieve their goals. Whatever you do, build a habit so that your review of the past day and planning for the next are done before 9:00 a.m. By 9:00 a.m. the world is up, and they will be trying to get hold of you. Many agents fail because they miss this one habit.

You should also create habits around family, sleep, and exercise. My best time for exercise is 3:30 p.m., and my body loves it. So it is in my calendar every day. Listen to the rhythm of your body and build your exercise habits around it. Other habits I have developed include going to bed at the same time every night, eating dinner at the same time, and spending time with my kids every evening. My wife and I also have a date night on the same day every week. Building habits around the big goals you have set will naturally propel you toward achieving them.

Habits also save you from decision fatigue. Our brains only have so much space for decisions, self-control, and critical thinking. Every morning we wake up with a full bucket of brain power, and every decision we make takes a little bit of that power away. It's like a battery—the more you use it the faster it loses its charge. Decision-making and critical thinking take a lot of brain power. This is one of the reasons why habits are so powerful: they do not take up brain space. They do not require decision-making, self-control, or critical thinking. The more habits I have, the more I can save my brain power for prospecting, client service, and all the problem-solving required of salespeople. Realtors underestimate the amount of mental effort it takes to find new clients and to be on your game for your current clients. Our job is anything but routine, so we need to find a way to gain as many habits as possible. Developing habits will help you overcome decision fatigue, increase your productivity, and elevate your career.

Micro-commitments are slightly different than habits. Habits are the same thing every day while micro-commitments are the first step required to move you in the direction of those habits. They work together beautifully. Micro-commitments are bite-sized and manageable steps to achieving big goals. They take a big goal and turn it into a daily goal. A micro-commitment can be as easy as calling five past clients a day rather that saying you will call one hundred people per month. If calling past clients is a hard task for you, then you need to turn it into a habit and a micro-commitment. The habit will be adding five people to your task list every day in your planning session, and the micro-commitment will be making just the first call. If you make the first call, the others become easy.

I have seen micro-commitments help me succeed in my running goals. I love to run, and I love the feeling after a run, but starting the run can sometimes be hard. My inner-self would rather sit on the couch and drink beer. I overcome this temptation with a micro-commitment: I tell myself to just get to the parking lot where I start my run and lace up my running shoes. When I get this far, without fail, I end up going for my run. This is a powerful tool to help you succeed in real estate. If you want to knock on doors but feel overwhelmed, then set a goal to knock on one door, and suddenly the rest will be easy. Maybe you need more clients in your database but never seem to get around to adding them: set a micro-commitment of adding a few clients every day. If you add three, or even one, a day you will have a database of thirty to ninety people in one month. If you are "stuck" in any area of your life, give yourself daily micro-commitments, and meeting the big goals will follow.

Micro-commitments are also great for building confidence. When we complete even the smallest task, it helps build confidence and confidence is key in sales. A realtor who lacks confidence will struggle to sell homes. It is easy to fail at big goals, but it is just as easy to succeed at micro-commitments. So if you are lacking confidence, you need to reset and focus on accomplishing small tasks and not worry about the large ones. Instead of focussing on the large goal of selling a house, focus instead on the process of getting there. In other words, focus on the process instead of the results. I have this painted on the front wall of my office so every agent will see it when they walk in. Process over results will boost your confidence and have you reaching goals you never thought possible.

Setting goals will be a game changer in your life. I feel like when you put a goal into the universe and work towards it, the results seem to fall in place. I can't tell you how many times I have set a goal, and at the end of the year I have come incredibly close to achieving it. It will be the same for you. I dare you to try. There are many goal setting resources available at www. elevatecoachingco.com.

Final Thoughts

Real estate can be the best career in the world if you apply yourself properly. Hopefully this book can act as your guide to stay on the right path from the start of your journey to the end. Remember this book is only a guide and will not guarantee success unless you put in the effort. Only you can take the words and turn them into actions. You are going to hit a lot of obstacles in your journey if you are lucky. These challenges will come from both people and circumstances. Don't be surprised and reactive when they happen, instead, try your best to learn from them and move on. Anyone that hits any level of success will gather a certain number of jealous haters. It's a sad fact, but it's true. Mother Theresa said it best: "People are often self-centred, illogical and unreasonable. Forgive them anyway...If you are kind, people may accuse you of selfish, ulterior motives. Be kind anyway...If you are honest and frank, people may cheat you. Be honest and frank anyway....If you find serenity and happiness, they may be jealous. Be happy anyway. The good you do today may be forgotten tomorrow. Do good anyway. Give the world the best you have, and it may never be enough. Give your best anyway. For you see, in the final analysis, it is between you and your God. It was never between you and them anyway. "

Please remember my favourite acronym: MEDC (Make Every Day count). If you can put in the daily effort every day and believe you are making it count, it will. The productive days will turn into productive weeks, the productive weeks will turn into years, and suddenly decades will go by. You won't notice the difference, but people around you will. Your growth will be so steep that you will barely recognize the person you used to be. If every day has a purpose, you will do incredible things. Anything you put your mind to can be achieved. Remember, selling real estate is simply the bus that gets us to where we want to go. So figure out where you want to go, and take action. This is your life and your career so take responsibility for everything you do. You just need to be the person of action. If you are anything like me, you will want everything now. Even when you make every day count you won't notice the small wins building immediately, so have patience with yourself. Patience is a virtue after all. Success doesn't come overnight, it takes time. I once ran into this older businessperson that I looked up to, and I told him that I wish I could be doing as much as he was doing. He paused, then smiled, then looked at me and said, first you crawl, then you walk, and then you run. I felt a bit annoyed when I heard this, but it was the most accurate advice he could have given me. I was acting daily and on the right path, but I still had so many steps to learn (and still do). You cannot skip the steps and must learn every lesson along the way. We are way more capable than we think, its only our minds that limit us. The universe has nothing but room for you to have an amazing story.

Finally, it is important to surround yourself with great people. I believe people are better together and human connection is one of the greatest gifts. Find people who inspire you, encourage you, and challenge you all in all aspects of life. It is important to be a coach and be coached. The goal is to be learning and teaching at the same time. The world is so connected right now you can find people from across the globe to be in your tight circle. If you are lucky enough to have incredible people in your life you will be better for it. I have had some of the most amazing mentors in my journey so far, and I hope to be a mentor for the rest of my life. I am the person I am because of the great people in my life who put the effort into spending time with me. We can learn from everyone to have an attitude of curiosity always. Be grateful, be humble, be careful who you surround yourself with, and make every day count.

Thanks for reading this book! I hope it was instructive, inspiring, and a guide to help you on your journey. I am excited for the places you will go.

BIBLIOGRAPHY

Accurate colour lives here (no date) *Home: Colour Communications, LLC:* Available at: https://ccicolour.com/ (Accessed: 28 November 2023).

Employee tenure summary - 2022 A01 results (2022) *U.S. Bureau of Labor Statistics.* Available at: https://www.bls.gov/news. release/tenure.nr0.htm (Accessed: 28 November 2023).

Jones, J.M. (2021) *In U.S., 40% get less than recommended amount of sleep, Gallup.com.* Available at: https://news. gallup.com/poll/166553/less-recommended-amount-sleep. aspx#:~:text=Americans%20currently%20average%20 6.8%20hours,health%20problems%20and%20cognitive%20 impairment. (Accessed: 28 November 2023).

More isn't always better (2014) *Harvard Business Review.* Available at: https://hbr.org/2006/06/more-isnt-always-better (Accessed: 28 November 2023).

Professions with the highest rates of alcohol abuse (2023) *Alcohol.org.* Available at: https://alcohol.org/professions/ (Accessed: 28 November 2023).

Quick Real Estate Statistics (2015) *www.nar.realtor.* Available at: https://www.nar.realtor/research-and-statistics/quick-real-estate-statistics (Accessed: 28 November 2023).

Your attention didn't collapse: it was stolen (2022) *The Guardian.* Available at: https://www.theguardian.com/science/2022/jan/02/attention-span-focus-screens-apps-smartphones-social-media (Accessed: 28 November 2023).

www.brainyquote.com/quotes/will_durant_145967

https://insideoutmastery.com/new-years-resolution-statistics/

https://quixy.com/blog/social-media-statistics-for-every-channel/

Printed in Canada